Holistic Philosophical Studies
Presents

Direct Democracy

Part 2 in the Series for the Humanist Element of the Square

by,

Michael Stansfield

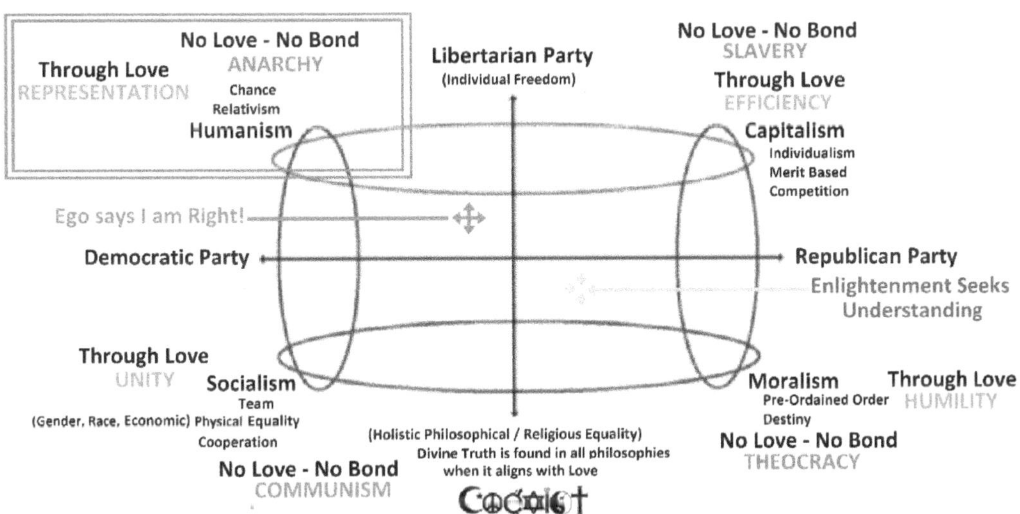

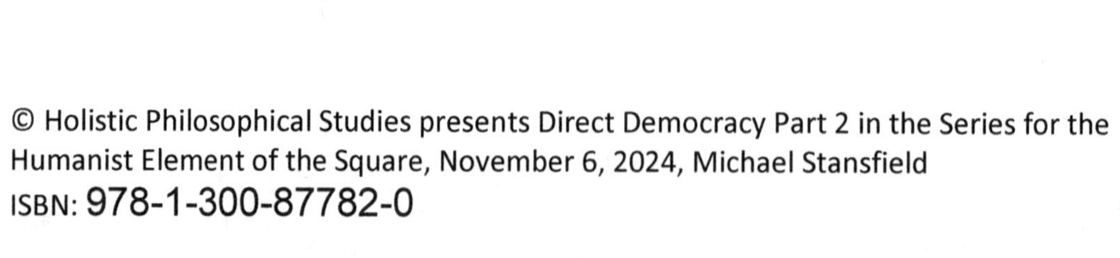

ISBN: 978-1-300-87782-0

TABLE OF CONTENTS

for the Humanist

It is always easier to fight for one's principles than to live up to them.

-Alfred Adler

Direct Democracy

Part II – (Dedicated to the Humanist Element of the Square)

Introduction

Before a child learns how to speak, they often get frustrated with the inability to express what they want. The frustration often leads to tantrums and screaming. Anger is a cry for help when one believes their needs are ignored, pushed aside, treated as trivial, or neglected. In the previous section, I discussed the need for us to find our true selves and use that essence through love to propel humanity forward. Yet in a world of billions of people most of us feel like that child, frustrated and angry because each see needs within humanity, but to one degree or another feel voiceless to make a tangible difference. This voicelessness in the long term is destructive for humanity individually and holistically as many have turned to ruthless and desperate actions to make themselves heard. This struggle for the representation of *we the people* is as old as the human race and though it is not taught in the Tanakh, the Gospel, or the Quran, it is just as vital to the evolution of our species. This road, like humanity's religious struggle, has been equally bigoted and bloody. For instance, as enlightened as the first republic in Rome was, it was also racist as only Roman Citizens could be members of the Roman Senate and yet those who made it into the inter-circle of power, as Julius Caesar testifies to, murder and other underhanded tactics were commonplace. Have we truly evolved as a society? Apartheid existed in South Africa through the 1980s. And most Evangelical Christians and Orthodox Jews still advocate for segregation between Jews and Palestinians in Israel. Yet racism and bigotry are not the only elements that deny representation to the people. There is also wealth and privilege (as the Arabs call it wasta). Beyond that, the party system itself becomes an impediment to imagination and creative ideas that fit outside of the binary party box.

In our modern political process, each candidate is sent a plethora of surveys for where they stand on issues. The questions are leading based on the direction the lobby desires. Each question is given an option yes or no, but if the candidate wished to clarify their answers, they are given no more than twenty characters so that either they can give a party-line sound bite, or their opinion is left out of the equation altogether giving the public the impression that they were unwilling to take a stand on the issues. Furthermore, the party is looking for people that will vote for and or against whatever the party's wishes are, so if one is willing to be their puppet, they will have a host of people making phone calls and all sorts of other things on their behalf, but such politicians are not truly working for the people, but rather the party and/or special interests financially backing them. Lobbying firms want commitments from candidates on various pieces of legislation, so that the politicians are bought off through public endorsements before even being elected to office. Of course, their endorsement depends greatly on one's bank account and or popularity, as their true goal is to piggyback their agenda through the candidates' campaign. The party structure for each state is run through its governor and the opposing gubernatorial candidate who each selectively supports candidates for the state legislature who they believe will be subservient to their wishes. Once elected only the legislators who prove their loyalty advance as candidates to congress as the president and/or presidential candidates are also only seeking to advance candidates who will be subservient to their wishes as they themselves are subservient to their doners. Thus, it should come as no surprise when evil is found at the top, none, or at least very few in congress are willing to step out of line for the moral high ground, even when that moral high ground is saying no to suppressing speech, insurrection, and even genocide, because they have been taught over and over again such stands against leadership are typically fatal to one's career. The result is that the mouth of the politician is paid to manipulate public opinion in the interest of the party and their donors rather than to represent their constituents. Rather than accountable to the electorate each politician is reading from the same talking points using the same stereotypical sound bites that speak directly to what the people within their philosophy want to hear to defame their political opponent and their cause with little to no in-depth discussion of the topics, thus denying growth and evolution to their own political party and amplifying the political tension in society. So, then the difficult reality comes to the surface. Where is the place for humanity to hear the undesired truth? In the religious world we spoke about the great need of the religions to understand and know one another. The need in the political world is just as great. Hate requires an opponent to exist, and the party system cannot exist without an opponent, whereas love sees the beauty in all and champions all. Buddha understood what it meant to be both rich and poor, but in knowing both an enlightenment was achieved that neither the Capitalist nor the Socialist could fully grasp. Prophets of love see and become all, but in becoming all a new philosophy is born within them, how to represent the whole without divisiveness so that each feels accepted and a part of the solution for a greater humanity. Given that need, how can the common person willing to testify to that truth, without wealth or popularity, have a voice in a political system that thrives on division? To solve this dilemma my task is to open the eyes of humanity to a new Tao, a political consciousness to bring the fullness of that representation to all. Yet just as the structure of our religious institutions create walls and boundaries that prevent them from achieving transcendence, our political structure itself also creates walls and boundaries and amplify that hate. Thus, I am left with the task to conceptualize a system that is altogether different from the political and economic reality of the present. For a world with limited imagination such endeavors are as impossible as bringing together the Jew, Muslim, and Christian, but I am here to plead on behalf of the Human Spirit. To put your hope, not only in God, but also in each other and all.

The tools of the Humanist are history and endless opinions about ideas, from all philosophies and, dare I say it, religions; creatively shaped, transformed, tested, and rearranged continually through the power of our God-given imagination, wisdom, and character. Muhammad asserted, "He who goes forth in search of knowledge is considered as struggling in the cause of Allah[1] *and* wisdom is the lost property of the believer, let him claim it wherever he finds it.[2]" We are not called to be ignorant of

---

[1] Sunnah.com Book 13; Hadith 10
[2] Hadith on Knowledge

the ideas of man, but rather to know their place. For all philosophies, whether they be conservative, liberal, libertarian, communist, or a thousand others, are they not all religions in their own unique right? Do they not all taint our perspective of humanity and the world? I ask this so that the reader will not consider what part someone else may be tainting, but rather for self-evaluation of his or her own thoughts and ideas. Nor do I mean to imply that to have a bias in our perception is always wrong, though it can be. There is a balance. For our Designers created us to think, to ponder, to aspire, and intentionally designed each of us with the ability to think intuitively, through our own perspective, yet to also hold rational judgment over our conclusions. The would-be gods of this world are not like our God;[3] they would have humanity follow their perspective alone and *cast-aside* all other points of view, even and commonly through war, violence, and bloodshed. My personal struggle is to achieve a government where the people themselves are not *cast-aside*; rather, it would be a world without limitations imposed on anyone's unique imagination.

Now *we* (myself, you the reader, and all who have an ear to hear and break the chains of tyrants) are about to embark on a journey to free humanity, to experience its natural and preordained intended destination. This is a struggle that did not start with me but goes back to the beginning.

Direct-Democracy

Thomas Jefferson was one of the leading voices advocating for the direct-representation of the cast-aside[4], as FDR would phrase it the forgotten man. This is not a question of how to represent the majority or the minority, but how to represent each person individually as a minority of one[5]—the concept that we call democracy. Today many refer to this word all the time, especially in the United States, but the United States is not a true democracy. As we may recall from the U.S. Pledge of Allegiance, "We pledge allegiance to the flag and to the republic for which it stands . . ." America, and most of the world, for that matter, has a republican form of government. The word *republic* comes from the Latin word *respublica*, which translates to *publica* ("public") plus *res* ("thing"), or *public thing*. A republic also has a form and a structure that come along with it, which people today are able to relate to and visualize, whereas when people imagine true democracy, they picture a large group of citizens discussing the issues and concerns of a local community, and then the whole community votes, issue by issue, as was done in ancient times. In Tiananmen Square, on May 29, 1989, a group of Chinese students protesting communism constructed a figure known as the *Goddess of Democracy*, modeled and fashioned after the Statue of Liberty.[6] As the protests became more and more widespread, the students realized that they had a fundamental problem. They had this idea called *democracy*, which they had learned about from America. Based on the American ideals echoed by Jefferson, each person has a voice in his or her government, but they had no practical way to achieve that political ideal. Suddenly, they came face-to-face with the real political problem of how to achieve their political

[3] Psalm 82

[4] Luke 22:25–27.

[5] Judges 17:6, 21:25.

[6] See <en.wikipedia.org/wiki/Goddess_of_Democracy>.

ideal. Democracy, unlike a republic, has no realistic or practical model that works well with large-scale populations. Yet Jezreel is the prophetic government of the Prince's kingdom that unites the Global South.

Historically, there have been several reasons for the development of this apparent impasse. The term *democracy* comes from the Greek word *demoskratia*, which means *demos* ("people") *kratia* ("to rule"), or, literally, *people to rule.* Republics allow for a small group of people to devote their time and energy to the passage of laws, and this enables the rest of the people to go about the normal business of their daily lives. Ancient democracies often changed drastically, like the weather, depending on who was attending the meetings. As populations increased, the bureaucratic nightmares and obvious inefficiencies of this simple form of government soon became patently obvious. After all, how could we possibly expect each and every person in the Global South—with its estimated six billion (as of 2024)—to have any real voice in his or her government? Legislatures and city councils also pass routine budgets for higher education and local schools and military expenses, and then there are traffic and safety laws, roads, and bridges to maintain; sewage and trash disposal to oversee; schools, clinics, and hospitals to run; urban development to control and zone properly; as well as other standards, protocols, local customs, traditions, and municipal regulations to observe, all of which can involve highly technical matters or various kinds of expertise and experience to address properly and which would be inefficient and impractical for society as a whole to ever hope to monitor, police, and control.

While we analyze these problems with direct-representation, we might wonder what Jefferson's solutions were, and why would Jefferson encourage such radical political ideas? Thomas Jefferson was an idealist. He knew what he wanted, but he did not always have a realistic, practical plan to achieve his political ideals. He did have a general set of principles that he knew were essential in order to achieve any truly democratic government. For instance, he knew that democracy, if it were really ever to be achieved, must begin with local government and from there work its way upward to the higher levels of government and, in this way, stay as close as possible to the people and their wishes. As he said, *"The hand of the people . . . has proved that government to be the strongest of which every person feels himself a part."*

There were, however, questions that Thomas Jefferson could not answer. His solution rested in the fact that one day, eventually, answers would emerge with the help of advancing technology and philosophy, that the people, through their own inherent instincts and demands to enhance their own representation, would have another revolution, or they would have many revolutions. In fact, Jefferson saw revolution itself as an essential part of the democratic process. Revolution, as he understood it, was part of the natural evolution of a free society: *"A little rebellion now and then is a good thing . . . the tree of liberty must be refreshed from time to time with the blood of patriots and tyrants."*

In historical terms, Jefferson saw and understood the U.S. Constitution as only one step in a long evolutionary development of democracy and its natural process and not as the finished, final, perfect, whole, complete, transcendentally good institution that it tends to be viewed as today. That is to say, Thomas Jefferson saw the different aspects of the Constitution merely as theories or temporary working hypotheses, rather than as anything permanent, such as natural laws. In time, he thought, theories would once again be put forward, continuously debated, and finally acted and improved on, until a finer, truer democracy would emerge: *"The ground of liberty is to be gained by inches, [and] we must be contented to secure what we can get from time to time, and eternally press forward for what is yet to get. It takes time to persuade men to do even what is for their own good. At the formation of our government, many had formed their political opinions on European writings and practices, believing the experience of old countries, and especially of England, abusive as it was, to be a safer guide than mere theory."*[7]

Notice that he says, "eternally press forward," not looking back, as Lot's wife did.[8] People tend to imagine that what they once knew long ago—possibly in some remote place now commonly invested with the aura of a mythical golden age—is somehow inherently superior to their own present conditions and possibilities. Thus, political theories advanced long ago by Thomas Jefferson produce in our own time a seemingly insurmountable challenge, if we are to eternally press forward. For Jefferson's day and the political prejudices of that era, the U.S. Constitution may have seemed to many the best possible document they could manage, but today, with the fading of the horse and carriage, muskets, and sailing ships, does such a possibility to achieve Jefferson's ideals still endure? Nevertheless, still many Christians in the modern era place the US Constitution on an equal level with the Bible.

This brings us directly to the struggle that most people have with the Mosaic Law as many Orthodox Jews and Puritans see the Torah (the law of the Old Testament) not as the beginning of law in antiquity, but rather the final perfection of law because it was written by God. The same could be said for Muslims would support Sharia law. This is not in any way meant to be a challenge to the laws established through God.[9] Rather than an end in and of themselves, I believe, the laws of God set up a foundation that human study and aspirations can build on.[10] Consider the earth, the foundation of God's creation, which sustains our very existence, yet Love granted humanity complete control over the earth.[11] This control, however, is limited to the laws of nature and science put in place by our Creator.[12] Through God's divine nature, the divine imagination within each plant and animal through the eyes of the microscope yields worlds and forms of life that continue infinitely smaller than the human eye could ever see, to the telescope, allowing us to ponder the massive expanses and universes beyond our grasp, Our Creator has left humanity an infinite journey into the discoveries of the creativity of God. The logic and wisdom of the mind of humanity are continually finding other unique and elegant aspects of creation, each at a preordained time, that God will grant to humanity,[13] a time when humanity is ready to receive them, for scripture tells us that there is a Day of Jezreel,[14] a day when the

---

[7] In Defense of Democracy, <etext.virginia.edu/jefferson/quotations/>, Letter to William Stevens Smith (November 13, 1787), quoted in Padover's *Jefferson on Democracy*, <en.wikiquote.org/wiki/Thomas_Jefferson>.

[8] Genesis 19:24.

[9] Books of the Law (Genesis, Exodus, Leviticus, Numbers, Deuteronomy).

[10] Joshua 1:8; Psalms 1:1–3, 119:96–97.

[11] Genesis 1:28.

[12] Jeremiah 33:25.

[13] Jeremiah 17:10.

[14] Hosea 1:11.

cast-aside will be given a voice in the world. What began with the establishment of the law[15] evolved to the rule of kings,[16] which our Preordainers declared ahead of time would take place.[17] The monarchies had their day until the rise of the Republics. Yet in our world of Republics, that pride themselves for their freedoms and liberties, we documented in the previous chapter how the voice and cry of the Palestinians and Arab people were muzzled, pushed into the darkness through stereotypes, bigotry, stubborn, unconcerned hearts unwilling or desiring to listen. Of course, this goes beyond the debate over the Arab identity to all who challenge the established order of our world. Of what value is free speech in societies that have been programmed not to listen, programmed for what is possible and what is not possible? So because I am challenging the impossible, I am faced with the dilemma of the human heart. It is not enough to say that all the elements within the Competitive Square of Humanity must be given a voice. I must provide humanity an avenue through which that voice and open dialog may be achieved. For we have already established there is a preordained day when the republic form of government will fade away upon the light of the coming day of Jezreel[18]—this, our God-given challenge that the light within us, as within all of humanity, should shine[19] and bring us out of these dark ages. After taking on such a challenge of further evolutionary democratic development, we must go beyond that early provisionary foundation of the republican system of government to the next level of a government based on direct, not indirect, representation. Our challenge is that now the overall look and feel of the system must be altered to such an extent that some of the foundational structures of government itself need to be redesigned. The purpose of Jezreel is that the voice of the voiceless will be heard, by which Love will respond with grain, new wine, and oil.[20] To accept this challenge, we must create a governance model based on direct-representation of the cast-aside and make direct-representation suitable for large-scale populations, for a civilization as numerous as the sands of the seashore and the stars of the sky.[21] To do this, we may begin by putting theories about the republic to the test, now that we have seen in action many modern examples of the republic as a form of government. By doing so, we can learn from a historical point of view which theories have worked well and which have not. Ultimately, it is we who must determine which, if any, practical options are available to meet the Jezreel political challenge and if indeed such a system of government can function well, safely, and securely, by the same standards we use to measure our present republican forms of government.

For Americans, Jefferson's political ideas seem to represent everything that America stands for, and people repeatedly quote him and his ideas about government—its foundation, structure, and purpose—as if they have all been fully achieved and are, in fact, fully embodied in their current government. However, the fact remains that unless we are willing to do everything possible to meet the political ends he and the founding fathers of America once envisioned, we will never bridge the divide to reach humanity's fated Promised Land. We must recognize that our collective historical

---

[15] Exodus 20.

[16] 1 Samuel 8.

[17] Deuteronomy 17:14.

[18] Hosea 1:11.

[19] John 1:4.

[20] Hosea 2:22.

[21] Genesis 22:17.

ideas about democracy, which are now thousands of years old, having survived two and a half millennia from ancient Greece, have in fact evolved with practical experience, making it increasingly possible now for many or most of the problems historically associated with direct-representation to be overcome. Yet although the basic goals of ancient democracies and this new form of direct-representation may be the same, our methods must be radically different if we are to be successful.

In today's political environment, in order for a person to achieve his or her political ambitions and have a significant voice in his or her society, this individual must depend on an elected representative in order to bring his or her idea before the legislature, the Parliament, or the Congress for a vote. Jezreel's hope for posterity was to create a political system of direct-representation, wherein each and every person is given the authority to represent one's self. For our, King has revealed to us that within each one of us, there is a light, a dream, and an aspiration that burns in our very soul. He wanted us to let our light shine,[22] for there is a light within humanity.[23] We know that governments that let the light of their people shine, in some degree, thrive, grow, and prosper, and we also know that governments that suppress this light oppress their people, and eventually they fail. We saw this, for instance, when the Berlin Wall was torn down and then with the collapse of the Soviet Union's communist regime. As has been true in the past and will be true in the future for many political scientists, when the world hears about this claim for a coming new Arab World, where each person can have a direct voice in his or her own government, even with populations of millions or billions to come, surely people will think that I must not be in my right mind. Yet haven't they already suggested this when I informed the world that the Arab people are Love's chosen people[24] and a holy nation?[25] Nevertheless, the promise of Love remains, that Jezreel serves to pave the way for a governmental model of real democracy, which today political science professors refer to as *direct-democracy*, and this is the political end that has been sought for countless generations, one after another. In fact, it is what we have always wanted, and now we can have it.

During my college years, while attending classes in political science, I was taught, as was the standard practice among political science scholars, that *direct-democracy* is simply not possible or practical with today's nations and their large-scale populations,[26] but this is needlessly limited thinking, and it is contrary to everything I know about science. By *science*, in this book, I refer to the scientific method as a means of discovery.

As I began to do more political science research, I came to realize that even with all the prestige of science and scientific learning, today we are only in the infancy of this scientific journey. The ancient Roman philosopher Seneca said, *"To each new generation, Nature reveals some secrets,"* and *"We imagine that we are Nature's chosen initiates or her most favored students, but in reality, we are only standing about in the anteroom, or foyer, and have not yet entered into the inner sanctum."*

---

[22] Matthew 5:16-17.

[23] John 1:4.

[24] Deuteronomy 7:6, 14:2; 1 Kings 3:8.

[25] Exodus 19:6, Leviticus 20:26, Deuteronomy 26:19; 1 Peter 2:9.

[26] "The United States Is a Republic," speech by Senator Byrd—"which a republic has over a democracy, in controlling the effects of faction," <byrd.senate.gov/speech-repub.htm>.

Also, please do not be surprised to learn that I, too, have questions and even some uncertainties about my own theories, but this is only natural with all forms of science and scientific discovery. To imagine that there is really any such thing as *establishment science* would be a paradoxical contradiction in terms, for science itself is the scientific method, which is a way to question carefully our presently held assumptions and in that process, learn more about the laws of nature. It was this overriding personal need I had to unravel Jezreel's riddle that, long ago now, ignited my quest. After all my years on this quest, I can now tell you this for certain: Jezreel (direct-democracy) is not only possible but is a far more practical and realistic form of government and better for our day and age than is the republic, which has seen its time. It is time for a change because Jezreel is God's intended Kingdom of Heaven destiny for those of us willing to enter the promised land. That is why I write, and that is, quite simply, the purpose of this book. For these changes must come about through and by humanity. I do not claim any divine inspiration for the government model I present. I say this so that none should fear challenging or modifying the ideas proposed, for this work is a task given to all humanity. Through the natural evolution of various forms of government, the time is ripe, and this is an idea whose time has come as if it were preordained. The nineteenth-century American poet Walt Whitman saw this coming as long ago as 1860 when he wrote: *"We have frequently printed the word 'Democracy, ' yet I cannot too often repeat that it is a word the real gist of which still sleeps, quite unawakened. . .. It is a great word, whose history, I suppose remains unwritten, because that history has yet to be enacted."*

To Whom Much Is Given . . .[27]

There was a time when the greater part of humanity believed that the earth was flat, and the sun revolved around it. We would laugh at any who would hold such beliefs today, and yet it wasn't so long ago that everyone knew Saddam was hiding weapons of mass destruction. Everyone knew that enhanced interrogation techniques at Abu Ghraib were stopping terrorist attacks. While all of these were false society deemed them true because they were repeatedly told so by those they put their trust in. In the section for the moralist, I went through the Bible to show how misrepresented God is. How even to ask legitimate questions that lend the hint that God loves Muslims leads to censorship and expulsion. Even elementary research on the Bible, the oldest and most prolific book on the planet invites questions that Zionism cannot answer, and yet even in the modern enlightened era Zionists, be they Christian or Jew, are actively committing genocide and would rather die than accept the Arabs as their lost brother Joseph. They hold to a religion built on faith in God to fulfill His promises and then deny His foundational precept upon which all faith is built, the fulfillment of the Abrahamic Covenant through the resurrection of Israel. At nauseum I would see those at the altar praying, pleading to understand God, nevertheless when any approached them with new perspectives on God they were impaled by these same people as heretics. If Democracy was about the will of the majority all these inaccuracies would become law and the creativity of humanity to seek out new and different ideas would grind to a halt. Yet this has already taken place, in all the

[27] Luke 12:48.

instances written and many more the religious zeal of society's ingrained beliefs is already censoring media and arresting college students for speaking out on the plight of the children of Abraham actively being placed on the proverbial cross in Gaza. Thus, Democracy, at its core, must be about the rights of the one, not the majority. Among these rights denied are those that are the most sacred of all: the freedom of speech, freedom of religion, freedom of self-expression, freedom of the press, freedom of assembly, even the most elemental right, the right to live. Seeing its denial of the most basic liberties for the crime of merely existing, we must turn it around to provide the maximum God-given rights to every man, woman, and child, whether foreign or native without discrimination. It is important to remember that Love is going to restore the children of Abraham, not because of their works, nor from any genetic goodness or superiority, but rather to show the holiness of his great name.[28]" Still, we should also realize that direct-democracy, like our present republic, is not an ultimately complete, finished, and perfect form of government. Like all things, science and the ambition of humankind will never cease challenging, inventing, or creating. Democracy in its elemental form relies upon the common people, the cast-aside[(Jezreel)], to affect the minds of the many, expecting them to make the right and most correct decisions for their societies. When one comes to understand this, then one knows that voting is indeed a privilege, not a right. That is, it is not a privilege based on land ownership, wealth, or power, but rather it is (or should be) a privilege based on social maturity and moral character.[29] As we look at the first of these elements, social maturity,[30] we understand that there are individuals that are not yet ready for this responsibility, because they have not reached an age of socially mature understanding.

A young child can be taught many things, but until he or she has reached an age of mental maturity, it may be difficult for the child to understand theoretical concepts concerning policies of the government. Similarly, in much the same way, a child needs its parents to survive, learn, and grow to that certain age when it is ready to move out into the world on its own.[31] Think of it in these terms: If one were to remove a six-year-old from his or her home—known from its earliest childhood—then the child most assuredly would not survive on its own.

We also understand that different people mature at different rates. Therefore, the freedom to alter or to make alterations to one's society depends on a person's social maturity to leave the nest and fly on one's own. Yet as foundations of any government are developed, one cannot say with certainty, when some particular person has reached such a general state of maturity. Thus, we need some standard or practical form of measurement that will show when and if a person has reached a general level of maturity. A point at which that person will be responsible and fully accountable for the decisions that will change, alter, and guide society. After all, if we were to ask a six-year-old boy if he is ready to be a man if he is anything like the boys I have known, he will always say that he is quite ready and eager to do just that, but reality turns out to be a different story. Ergo, for every goal we want to achieve, we

[28] Luke 12:48.

[29] Proverbs 12:2–3.

[30] Exodus 20:12; Deuteronomy 5:16.

[31] Proverbs 23:22–25.

need to develop practical application guidelines, including whatever is necessary to achieve that goal.

First, let's look at what it takes to fly. The first necessity for that is social maturity, as manifested by responsibility, courage, and self-reliance.[32] After all, it is only logical to assume that a person should not be making decisions about how society should function until he or she can function on his or her own in that society. In practical application terms, we can say that a person has reached this stage of development at the point of gaining full-time employment, attending college, or moving out of the parental nest. We can say this because each one of these achievements in its own way promotes responsibility, courage, and self-reliance, and it does so long-term, and in real ways. This is not intended to limit liberty, but rather enhance it. During the revolution, there was a saying, "No taxation without representation." Consider the following questions. Many sixteen-year-old youths are working twenty hours a week or more, and are they not also paying taxes and entitled to representation? On an academic level, we know there are gifted children known as prodigies. If these children are mature enough to attend and pass college-level courses at the age of twelve or thirteen, why should society believe that they are not capable of the responsibility to understand the issues in government competently? Now on the other side of the equation if a person is in good health, physically able to work, and yet is thirty-five never held of job or attended college, or at least some form of trade school, and is still living with their parents, can we really believe that such people should be guiding our society through the law-creation process?[33]

Of course, we know that there are exceptions to every such rule. Many people are physically handicapped and unable to work, others may be married, but living with parents to help raise their children while a spouse is in the military or away. In Arab cultures, united families of this type are the norm. Then there are other considerations, such as extreme economic depression when times are difficult, and it is very difficult to find work. These exceptions are important, and we have made note of them. However, our objective remains the same, to use the freedoms in society as a method to reward good behavior and have consequences for bad behavior.[34]

We also understand that there are people that may leave the nest of their childhood, but still be unable to fly on their own. People with drug addictions and other unhealthful dependencies, or certain abnormal mental conditions (depending on their severity), definitely may need help from their society, and should not necessarily become part of the decision-making process because their ability to do higher-level thinking has been measurably and all too often compromised.[35] Of course, the hope is that with time and the right treatment, they will one day be able to leave the prison cell of their dependency and become fully functioning, fully contributing members of society. However, there are shades of gray, even in this area. Those who are willing honestly and sincerely to look at themselves in a mirror and realize that they are struggling with unhealthful dependencies should not be penalized for seeking help. Therefore, we are drawing a distinction between those in a society that have been forced to deal with their dependency issues through

---

[32] Proverbs 6:6-11

[33] 2 Thessalonians 3:10

[34] Didache 1

[35] Matthew 7:6.

governmental law enforcement, such as, driving while intoxicated, apart from those who voluntarily and courageously seek help. We have deemed these citizens Dependent Class because they are dependent on society in some way, shape, or form.

Having said that there are jobs, such as pilots and bus drivers, that an employer may wish to put into dependent class level restrictions, not in terms of losing their right to vote, but in terms of not being able to purchase various types of alcohol or drugs, even though they may be legally sold in the area because they constitute a risk to the safety of their commercial clientele.

Our new constitution has set up this prototype class of citizenship as follows: (Remember that these Articles, as I will be presenting, are merely suggestions. The final constitutional wording will be established through the will of the people themselves. Also, note that some of the nuances of each Article may be explained in subsequent sections or chapters. Therefore, it is recommended that you do not read the Articles until the second read-through of this work so that you will be able to grasp the big and full picture of what we are attempting to achieve with Jezreel.

The most common present systems of representative government define this level of social maturity by age. At the age of eighteen, in most cases, a person is no longer tried in court as a child but rather as an adult.[36] Once a person turns eighteen, he or she may join the military, attend jury service, or even vote.[37] Also, a parent is no longer required by law to provide food and shelter to a sibling eighteen years of age or older. Yet are there not several real challenges with this too-simple method of determining legal maturity? First, it removes from the equation a person's actions. Social maturity, by definition, should be determined by a significant act, a series of significant acts, or other major character-driven events. Making social maturity an earned privilege, rather than an automatic entitlement, as has been proved historically, creates a powerful incentive for engaging in good, socially responsible behavior, which is then manifested in positive, practical results. We have deemed these citizens Independent Class because they have shown through their actions that they desire a privileged level of independence.

Unfortunately, there are persons in society that have proven by their criminal acts that they have not earned the privilege of being a part of society's decision-making processes.[38] This is not to say that they are unintelligent, but often their energy and purposes are not aimed at bettering our society or their neighbors, but rather, through deceptive manipulations to build a lesser subculture that they imagine will further their own selfish ends. Instead of being straight, positive contributors, their parasitic distortions turn aside or unhealthily distort the general good. For this discussion, because of their deeds, they have been removed from the decision-making process. Of course, our hope is that, through counseling and other forms of rehabilitation, at some point, these people may re-enter society, and through productive, good behavior be able to gradually regain their freedoms. Once again, we are determining a person's place in society based upon his or her significant acts, and once again, we must account for exceptions to rules. On the other hand, people

[36] Juvenile tried as an adult, <legalmatch.com/law-library/article/juvenile-tried-as-an-adult.html>.

[37] See the 26th Amendment, eighteen and the right to vote, <library.thinkquest.org/J0110162/18.html>.

[38] John 10:10.

can be—and sometimes are—imprisoned for intentionally violating laws they see as unjust.[39] About this, Martin Luther King Jr. said: *I submit that an individual who breaks a law that conscience tells him is unjust, and who willingly accepts the penalty of imprisonment in order to arouse the conscience of the community over its injustice, is, in reality, expressing the highest respect for the law.*

The nineteenth-century American transcendentalist author Henry David Thoreau became famous in part for his essay on civil disobedience, and this matter highlights the important logical distinction between natural moral laws, with also the idea of natural human rights, and man-made laws established by society, which is termed in political science *positive laws.*

Problems develop when there seems to be a basic conflict between natural and positive law, as in civil rights disputes. Due to the essential significance of this exception, and others as well, any failures, even to the smallest extent, in how matters are set up for law-creation in this better system of government—law-creation being the core element in any attempt to bring about direct-democracy—could ultimately undermine, erode, even dissolve the whole system. Therefore, the essential freedoms and civil liberties of the cast-aside person, the person *on the street*, must be the cornerstone of any attempt to bring about the Jezreel[(direct-democracy)] form of government.[40] All we have presently done is to set in place the natural boundaries in society on who should actively participate in the law-creation process. The first of these boundaries is social maturity because if a person is *to fly*, he or she must have the maturity to leave the nest. The second, after the bird has left the nest, it can spread its wings and fly on its own, while at the same not abusing someone else's right to life on the wing, which refers especially to those who have been convicted of crimes, which we have deemed Criminal Class Citizenship. Note that we have especially noted the basic rights of humanity in this lowest class of citizenship to ensure that these fundamental rights are held by all people.

For practical reasons, there must also be a third boundary. To participate in any democratic form of government, people must be citizens, either through birth or through the legal immigration process, before they may participate in the law-creating processes of democracy, and this is true of any nation on earth.[41] We have deemed these citizens Immigrant Class.

The political boundaries we have set up are not in any way new because societies, in one way or another, already have these boundaries in place. Our goal is to create a society without unreasonable boundaries for all who have proven by their actions that they are responsible adults who will not infringe upon the rights of others. Each one of us has a dream in our hearts, our Preordainers given goal that we long to reach and a path that we long to take.[42] Flying, in the simplest terms, is living that dream.

A republic as a form of government that unlike a direct-democracy, produces a fourth boundary, because the right to create and enact laws is not available to the average adult citizen, whether he is responsible or irresponsible. Inherent within it and by its very nature, it relies on elected persons known as *representatives* to represent and legislate the will of the people from the city, town, or municipality

---

[39] Acts 12:1–5, 16:22–24.

[40] Matthew 5:5; 1 Samuel 2:8; Psalms 37:11

[41] Exodus 12:49; 22:21, 23:9; Leviticus 19:33-34; 24:22.

[42] Exodus 4:10-12; Matthew 10:29; Luke 12:6–7.

where they were elected. However, when the elected representative fails to see his or her constituents as persons, each with their own different needs and values and starts seeing them instead as a whole body of people to be represented, then the core uniqueness and creativity inherent within each of us are lost. This is like the difference between walking along the ground and flying. In practical terms, being represented by one's representative means that a person must communicate by going to the representative. After telling that person one's opinions about what is wrong in that society, and what needs to be made right is then followed by hoping that the elected representative acts, sometime soon, on those concerns. Given the political right bestowed upon the representative by the governmental system, average people in society must go through them if they have any hope for a voice in the political process. This is a process that makes gods out of men.[43] Unfortunately, not all politicians are diplomats, and some turn out, after the elections, not even to be good people. With many, for one reason or another, the chances of being heard and of going this route to positive outcomes are rare, or slim to none. To see the most basic, foundational issues within the republic form of government, let's set aside for a moment the issue of the representative's moral character, with honesty and personal integrity (we hope), and assume that he or she has a good heart and will do the utmost to represent those constituents well, and for their highest good.

Does the core dream and passion in your representative's heart have the same scope, uniqueness, and creativity as your own? That is not to say that your representative's personal passion is any less beautiful or creative, but is it really just the same? One man's innermost passion may be medicine, another farming, or another auto mechanics.[44] It is this joy, this passion, this drive that makes us all fully human, as it brings out our creativity, and our unique personality, thereby leaving our own imprint on the world.[45]

This book and these ideas are my passion, my wings, and my joy! *No representative could express the desires of my heart as I do.* For this reason, in fact, throughout my life, I have studied politics and political systems. Who has the power, and how do things get done? Frankly, if I were your representative, I could only fail because I could never fully appreciate, comprehend, and then implement the creatively drawn inspiration of any other unique person through the lawmaking process, let alone the thousands upon thousands of people that compose a representative's hometown, district, or state. As the final irony in this picture, it is a representative's *sole responsibility* is to represent these people! This elemental fact and logical contradiction lie at the core challenge to the basic political principles facing all republics.

The Failures of Ancient Democracies

The founders of the Republican form of government were not blind to these issues, certainly, but they could see at the time no better way to fulfill the needs. This is not to say that they did not know about the historical democracies of the past eras, but

[43] Psalms 82, 4:2; Jeremiah 16:20.

[44] Abraham Lincoln, Communication to the People of Sangamo County, Illinois, March 9, 1832.

[45] "What Is Creativity?" by Linda Naiman, <creativityatwork.com/articlesContent/whatis.htm>.

rather that they declined a (directly) democratic form of government because they did study and then completely understand the democracies of the past, or why they had not been completely successful.

When most people think about democracy, they probably recall what they have learned about the early democracies of ancient Greece, in which communities got together to solve the issues that would arise from time to time. These meetings would take place in the morning, and superseded whatever other pressing needs the citizens of the community might have had. A difficulty about this governmental structure is that the citizens had the ability to alter totally the government's design and structure, and this gave those governments much instability. Because all political options could be chosen at any given meeting, some decisions were made rashly, without due consideration, dictated by the heat of the moment and the passing emotions of the discussions' speakers. Quiet, physically weak, or shy people would feel intimidated, and often the true democratic intentions and goals of this form of government were never brought to fruition as originally conceived. We know, for instance, about the tragic death of Socrates, and we know that Plato, from time to time, had his problems with the Athenians and their votes. The designers of the republics have voiced these same complaints about Jezreel[(direct-democracy)]. One of the most well-known of these designers was the fourth American president and father of the Constitution, James Madison. Madison once said: *Democracies have ever been spectacles of turbulence and contention; have ever been found incompatible with personal security, or the rights of property; and have in general, been as short in their lives as they have been violent in their deaths.*

The founders of Republican forms of government wanted the same goals of individual representation, but they believed it was impossible to achieve that without sacrificing safety, security, and stability. We also remember that besides Christ, some of history's greatest minds were ended or their work suppressed through the will of the people. Since the repercussions may be severe, the ability to create and pass laws and to bring about change in one's society is a responsibility not to be taken lightly. Like all things, if the creation of a direct-democracy form of government is not able to tackle the harsh criticisms leveled at it by its most ardent critics, or meet the high expectations of its most devoted advocates, then it will never last. The issue with direct-democracy from those who favor instead the republic form of government is the notion that Jezreel means mob rule.[46] There are several points to be drawn from this about how people go about the decision-making process.

The freedom to peaceably assemble and petition the government for a grievance is part of the US Bill of Rights, yet it's very use means that all other avenues for a voice in the system have been exhausted. Protestors are fed-up. In one way or another their voice is testifying that the system has already failed them to the point that they are willing to take to the streets to demand change. By the time people are marching on the capital they are beyond the point for any calm or rational discussion and any alteration to government that comes out of the heat of the moment is bound to fall

[46] Greek philosopher Plato, from his book, The Republic.<classics.mit.edu/Plato/republic.1.introduction.html>

as quickly as it came to rise. After a prolonged amount of time events such as those that took place on January 6th, 2021, were inevitable and unless representation evolves and expands such events are the first of many to come.

We could all agree, perhaps, that good decisions are based on sound data and research. To accomplish this, it becomes necessary to analyze an idea to its smallest, most seemingly minuet-detail, each considered carefully, with all the time necessary. Of course, all of this must take place in a safe, unthreatening environment, or any conclusions reached will be tainted. Bad decisions, on the other hand, tend to be those made during the heat of the moment, during intense argumentation. Bad decisions are also made when one feels coerced by arm-twisting or threatened in some way about the choices. The primary issue with these ancient, early democracies was that they were formed in such a way that their bad decisions were amplified and their good decisions were minimized,[47] which is exactly the opposite from the desired results of the democratic process. These systems were inefficient also because of the time and participation requirements placed upon the people within those governments. Besides that, those governments lacked stability, and therefore, they also lacked the kind of stable order necessary for healthy, long-term growth. With an ever-changing, in-flux government, people were unable to plan ahead sufficiently to conduct business.

For these reasons and for many others, which we will discuss in more detail later, truly democratic governments have for centuries ceased to exist. Gradually, with the passage of time, democratic institutions of government began to form that to some degree addressed the challenges faced by those first democracies. For example, one of those initiatives by genre was the state and local proposition, which made it possible for a person to place practical, specific ideas for change on the ballot. There were also other advances that enabled the cast-aside person to participate in town-hall meetings, to peaceably assemble, and to petition the government for redress, as well as other foundational freedoms of a democracy that most in the West know well, such as freedom of religion, freedom of speech, freedom of the press, and other such traditional Jezreel freedoms they currently enjoy and take for granted.

As we look at the first of these aforementioned institutions, state and local propositions, we notice several notable advances over how the early democracies worked. Part of this advancement was the way the propositions could amplify how the people could make sound, carefully deliberated decisions. Propositions, by their design and structure, place more emphasis on the individual and less on the group decision-making process. This meant that individuals could write law anytime they wished, without feeling pressured or threatened. Still, for a proposal to be placed on the ballot, a person has the monumental task of collecting enough ratifying signatures from the people in his city, shire, or state. To be precise in our terminology, the difference between a *proposal* and a *proposition* is that *a proposition has been placed on the ballot.* Then there are the months of decision-making time and debate within the electorate before the vote takes place. By making the law-creation process

47 Why democracy is a threat to liberty – "The smallest minority on earth is the individual" <angelfire.com/pa/sergeman/cliches/democracy.html>

longer, a society may take the time it needs to think, discuss, and debate all the various possible contingencies and options before the proposal reaches a final collective conclusion, which also thereby will diminish the challenges that come out of decisions originally made in the heat of the moment. This more deliberate process also limits the issues to a select few that the public sees as important, rather than leaving the debate wide open to all comers on the subjects at one sitting.

The propositions also break down the law-creation process into three unique and different steps as follows: (1) writing the proposals, (2) prioritizing the proposals and (3) passage of the proposals into law. Since each one of these elements—through the propositions—is derived from the people themselves, the people themselves remain mutually accountable to each other as individuals for the laws that they have passed together, as a group. With the capability of separating these processes into their individual, constituent elements, we are better able to analyze each element by itself, and better able to amplify the goals that they attempt to achieve. Also, we can understand better why the failure of the first democracies to separate these processes into their separate, constituent elements led to their downfall.

Step 1: The Writing of Proposals

Let us begin by studying the first element in the process, the writing of proposals. Every concept, discovery, or triumph of humankind may be thought of as having begun originally as some idea in some person's mind. That first passing thought, with its microseconds in the mind, is either dwelt upon further and accepted as such, or it is discarded. Today it is hard to imagine how many diseases would have been cured, or scientific discoveries made, from humanity's casually discarded thoughts. It was at this early stage in the early democracies that thoughts were expressed to the community at large with the purpose of altering the laws. This way of thinking about new initiatives was inherently problematic because the ideas presented were rarely researched, discussed, or challenged before they reached the open forum for public decision-making. The ideas that we want to mold into the formal proposals to be presented for the public's consideration are, by and large, only those that have been sifted and then cultivated with the most careful, painstaking research for days, weeks, or even years. They are the ideas that go on burning in a person's soul.

To accomplish this, we must begin by narrowing that single person's focus. By limiting a person to one proposal, until it is passed or fails by vote, that individual's attention is logically restricted to one primary area of study. That is not to say that they may not participate in all other aspects of the open democratic processes, but they should be restricted in the creation and sponsoring of specific new proposals.

Because one of our aims is to increase research and study, we must understand that research and study come in three forms. The first kind of research and study is that conducted by one person, the second kind of research and study is that conducted by a group and the third kind of research and study involves learning from the wisdom of others, such as in the classroom environment. These forms of research and study have been the cornerstones of serious, constructive thought throughout history, but all have been, and are, different in their applications. Therefore, our methods for designing proposals using these methods should also be different, to amplify their different individual strengths, depending on their needs and purposes.

The second method of an initiative developed through group work must deal with the complexities of group dynamics. If for a moment, we exclude individual research and study, then our only conclusion is that after an idea is dwelt upon, that idea's life will continue only if it is expressed, usually in words, to another person. After the thinker who originated the idea has passed on the idea to others, these others are faced with the same option, namely, either to dwell upon the idea or to discard it. For those who choose to dwell upon it, this is the time in the process when logic and reason are applied to the proposal, with its information, as presented. Now each person in the group has the opportunity, after due consideration, to come out with a conclusion based on his or her own logic, reasoning, and experience. Then, when a group agrees, they have a choice about whether they want merely to accept the situation as it is, or to pursue some change. However, a collective effort of one kind or another will be forthcoming only if the group (which is composed of individuals) is willing to make such an effort. Note that this is different from a collective thought because each of these individuals has, each one made a separate, personal decision to agree.

As research and study begin, the mind of each person is still operating independently, and the thought process of each person moves at will, in its own directions, and this process usually brings, in a familiar way, the disagreements that follow. Most of us would say that it is to be hoped that logic and reason will win the day, to reach the best possible results, but that is not always the case, and successful outcomes in the process depend greatly on the flexibility of the group's individuals. Of course, group dynamics dictate the need for flexibility, reasonableness, and ability to compromise, in terms of group numbers and composition, and depending on the environment and situation at hand.

In terms of the law-creation process, our groups, which we affectionately dub entmoots, will be made up of a sponsor and cosponsors. Entmoot, from the Dutch word, Entmoet, meaning to gather, is a mythical form of consensus building without time constraints where all ideas and opinions of descent are thoroughly considered and dwelt upon. For the purposes of discussion, a *sponsor* is the original author who contemplated and initiated the foundational idea. A *cosponsor* is a member of an entmoot consisting of the proposal sponsor, who may enlist other cosponsors, each of whom has voluntarily committed themselves to the specific single proposal, through the formal written agreement with the sponsor. As is typically the case the sponsors and cosponsors are like-minded individuals and because each sponsor and cosponsor have a large stake in the success of the proposal we are looking at a process of consensus rather than that of majority rule. Sponsorship or cosponsorship in a democracy, such as we are proposing, is available to all and restricted to none. Keep in mind that cosponsorship differs from an endorsement of a petition or proposal, as citizens may endorse any or as many proposals or petitions as they wish, however, each person is limited to the sponsorship or cosponsorship of one proposal until the proposal reaches the ballot or the entmoot is dissolved, of course, other exceptions do apply which we will discuss in time. Therefore, due to the commitment that the cosponsor has given to the proposal, each cosponsor, through legal written agreement, has the right to have his or her political voice expressed within the lines of the proposal itself as conscience dictates. Because of this, we can appropriately expect the sponsor of any proposal to be very selective when seeking out a cosponsor or multiple cosponsors for his or her political proposal. We should also consider that potential cosponsors might be hesitant to submit their fate to the proposal of another's passion, struggle, or cause. This may come about for several reasons. Some potential cosponsors may have a different perspective, which is incompatible with the sponsor, other potential cosponsors may themselves be unsure what areas they would like to pursue and are therefore hesitant or unwilling to commit to the proposal at that time. For these reasons and many others acquiring cosponsors who are qualified and reliable participants will be an arduous task. With all that in mind, the benefits of collaborative teamwork remain undeniable. Entmoot dynamics, when each member fills a lacking void in the entmoot itself, brings refinement and improvement to the proposal creation process by providing unique perspectives and shades of light to the idea, unseen or unrealized by the sponsor. While we allow sponsors to submit proposals without cosponsors, it is important for us to find ways to promote and encourage entmoot or cosponsorship of proposals to get the sponsor's ideas, *out of the box*, and avoid the potential for narrow-minded thinking.

To accommodate these needs, the more cosponsors exist in a proposal, the fewer petition endorsers are required for proposal submission. To accomplish this purpose, our general rule will be that if five or more cosponsors exist for proposals made through the entmoot decision-making process, then petition signatures from the community are not required to submit a proposal and begin our law-creation process. When a proposal is signed, the signer has no real consequences for submitting his or her signature, but the signer has no special privileges to modify the proposal itself, although a recommendation may be requested from the sponsor or cosponsor of the proposal. Conversely, the sponsor and cosponsors have the right to make any modifications they wish, but they are responsible for the modifications submitted. Therefore, the more sponsors and cosponsors a proposal has, the fewer signatures are required before the proposal may be taken to city hall; a sponsor and a cosponsor require eighty signatures before they may take the proposal to city hall; the sponsor and two cosponsors require sixty signatures; three cosponsors require forty signatures, and so on. Remember while these numbers apply to all communities equally this process is only the starting line, and actual endorsements required to place a proposal on the ballot will vary between communities as determined by population among other options. Through this deliberate design to encourage sincere collaboration, debate, and entmoot discussions in the proposal creation process, each of the cosponsors is tied to his or her own proposal, or they are all tied together collectively to some single proposal. This will be also a limiting factor on their liberty because they may sponsor or cosponsor only one proposal. We do this for many reasons, but primarily because we want to narrow the cosponsors' focus to the one idea, which will be the one research topic on the table for forum discussion.

The challenge with the vast majority of attempts to achieve direct-democracy is that the concept of the individual is ignored and the question is posed like this: "How can the will of the people be enacted when it is constantly changing?" The *will of the people*, in this case, refers to its collective thought, which is not possible to ascertain without exceptional telepathic power (which cannot be taught) to read other individual people's thoughts, and then to make up one's own mind to work as one with that other individual. This error comes into play when people attempt to combine all three independent parts of the process, as we have analyzed and discussed it, into a single amorphous, undifferentiated process. But this is not possible in our present-day and age, which instead insists upon posing as somehow real the illusionary flaws to which their confused thinking points as it attempts to relate to historical attempts at truly democratic governments.

The real question is not how one might be able to hear and then enact the collective people's voice, but rather, "How might one allow the cast-aside person to have a voice—a real voice—in his society?" If all people, as individuals, can have a real voice in his or her own government as individuals—a voice to express and alter all things that matter—then and only then would there be a true, real Jezreel.[48] Now that we have posed the core question, how can it be achieved?

In one way or another, all of us, through our childhood development, have used two methods of thought. In some cases, we learned through direct observation, and in others, we learned more indirectly, through others, such as from discussions with our family or friends. As you might have surmised, there was also a third option, for we might have learned collectively, through entmoot discussions. From a theoretical point of view, learning by direct observation often has many issues when, for example, one does not know or is not able to perceive all the facts of some given situation. This has led individuals to partially incorrect or even totally wrong, conclusions. In addition, a person may see a situation that seems to be headed for a bad conclusion, but their well-meaning intervention, like Don Quixote, may turn out to be ill-advised, leading to even worse or more complexly exacerbated conclusions. While most of us are not fighting windmills like Don Quixote, often we are deceived on facts through the media, teachers or even well-intentioned friends and family. Even when we have ninety-five-percent of our facts correct, the five-percent of the situation where we were error can change the entire outcome. Then there is the problem with our ego. At times, our emotions are so strong that we fail to see the truth, but rather only the facts as we wish to see them. This idea may sound complicated but, for example, Karl Marx was not incorrect about the social evils commonly built into the capitalism of his day and time, yet his proposed solution of communism produced more challenges than his supposed *solution* achieved. The truth is that Karl Marx did not want to see the good aspects of private enterprise, nor did he want to see the evils within government ownership. With the advantage of hindsight, we can say that these matters and many others like them, could have been dealt with much better if they had been thought about more carefully, with test cases and trial runs or pilot projects, before their massive, general application, and, as always, within the open forum of free debate and criticism.

---

[48] What is rational politics - <importanceofphilosophy.com/Politics_Main.html>

Yet the present system for initiatives and proposals has no way to tell a person or an entmoot whether the proposed idea is sufficient and workable at large, for the larger society. And then, too, we find ourselves within another major dilemma, for society never stops thinking, and it never stops developing, always with new ideas and new technologies, and therefore no idea has ever, nor will it ever, reach its absolute apex or ultimate pinnacle. To say that an idea could reach such a totally developed, maximum state is to say that technology and our creativity could reach a point beyond which our species could not travel, which denies science and human creativity there apparently infinite capacities for growth, change, and development. So then, realistically, with this open-ended scenario, while it is not possible to reach an infinitely or ultimately best-possible solution, still we need to attempt the creation of an environment wherein the optimal solution for each political issue may yet be, in some way, achieved.

When one stops to consider for a moment the most visionary minds our civilization has yet produced, it becomes apparent that no matter what the seemingly insurmountable challenges were at the time, they never stopped thinking about how to make their solutions better. Now, let's consider, as it currently exists, our present lawmaking process. First, someone writes a proposal. Second, that person collects the required number of signatures to get the proposition onto the ballot. Then, *after* collecting hundreds, a thousand, or many thousands of signatures some difficult challenge to—or much-needed improvement upon—the proposal is discovered. For all practical purposes and in most cases, it would be too late, for if the person changes the proposal, the signature gatherer loses all the signatures that were needed to put the proposal as designed onto the ballot. Therefore, feeling inevitably an obligation to all those who have signed already, the proposal becomes the proposition on the ballot as it was originally written—whatever that difficulty or shortcoming might be. We are dealing, then, with an unfortunate rigidity. The key is to provide the flexibility needed for the law proposer, as he or she understands the ideas most intimately, to change their proposal without an extreme loss to the signatures already gathered and at the same time ensure the people who have already signed the proposal are notified of all changes so that they remain involved in the creation process and can remove their signature if they so desire.

Due to these natural processes in the collective social development of ideas, for best results, the person or persons who develop proposals must reach what we may refer to as *completion of thought*, and this must happen *before* the signature-gathering process needed to place the proposal on the ballot has begun. There is an adage, *the speed at which you are going is less important than the direction in which you are moving.* Representatives in congress are elected every two years. This means all the proposals have a maximum of two years from being written to passage. Thus, time becomes the enemy of the legislator and amplifies the anxiety within the position. The goal of democracy is to take the urgency down a notch. This book, for instance, is decades of my carefree moments pondering existence and humanity, and yet each time I ponder issues here and there rise to the surface. Because as human beings we never stop learning. One will think they have a proposal completed, but let it sit for a while. After you have written it down let your mind forget. Move on to the necessities of life. Out of the blue if you don't revisit your ideas, eventually your ideas will revisit you. Something new will come to mind. Something that will enhance your idea. Thus, the dilemma. How do we amplify the process to transform satisfactory ideas, into exceptional ideas? To do this, we should further divide the proposal-writing process mentally into its real constituent subcomponents. The first subcomponent is the original idea or the spark of visionary insight in which the proposal has its original conception. The second subcomponent is the research done on an individual level or through the workings of an entmoot that develop and completely cultivate the original thought. After everyone in that entmoot—our cosponsors and sponsor—believe that they have reached a conclusion, or the individual studying on his own has successfully petitioned (for example) a hundred individuals in favor of a proposal, either the entmoot or the individual may then take the idea to the governing body, such as officials at city hall.

The Sage

Yet in all of this, we are still missing something. Everyone in the entmoot, or each of the persons who signed the petition, may be of the same general mindset, or of the same political persuasion. At some point, one needs an impartial third-party observer, which is not only our third option of learning but also our third sub-component. The political party system may have several issues, but the party system does create plausible counter-arguments and valid points of opposition to proposed rules, stipulations, regulations, or laws. Often, we humans have a habit of drifting into our own little fantasy world and imagining our ideas as already achieved, and, in the process, overlook, or even deliberately ignore valid, viable criticisms. Of course, this is not to say that people should be forced to take the recommendations and advice of others! To go that route would be to create a power base among advisers, who then become automatic revisers and correctors, thereby diminishing the innate, sovereign rights and powers of the common person. This overly cumbersome route could, in turn, eventually diminish the powers of the people themselves to the point where there is a real threat to the democracy itself. Still, it remains essential that a third-party individual or a nonpartisan group look over the proposals submitted for noting potential areas of concern, unforeseen contingencies, or to point out parts of the proposal that might not be clear. Obviously, these nonpartisan, uncommitted individuals must have some background knowledge and/or expertise about the issues under discussion. For example, one would not present a proposal on farming to a psychologist in the same way that one would not present a proposal on mental illness to a farmer, or an expert on agricultural economics. The institution to which a person or entmoot can go to have proposals studied must have available many various well-qualified, recognized experts—such as scholars, scientists, or engineers, for these formal consultations and critiques. A natural choice often might be some nearby or realm college or university, as here dubbed Fantasia. Many or most professors are experts in their chosen fields and normally would be able to do this job well, although they may sometimes lack necessary practical hands-on experience. This proposal review process might take some time, and patience will be required. Of course, in some kinds of situations, decisions must be made on the spur of the moment, such as in war and diplomacy, but that will be, here, one of our later considerations. Also, while it is true that the university system would be excellent for studying proposals, we must also realize that if we make it the only such source for such advice, criticism, and consultation, with that power source, we would also be producing a monopoly. Always we must remember that the government comes from the people. By placing the responsibility of each separate community upon itself to establish its own self-imposed but necessary restrictions and limitations, we also ensure that each government will grow, evolve, and make needed, common sense improvements upon itself as its circumstances will naturally require.

It is also expected and desired that after a person or entmoot has met with these independent advisors, they may want to revise their proposal and resubmit it to the independent advisors for another review. This process may occur several times, depending on the complexity of the proposal and the necessary knowledge, until the individual or entmoot feels assured that the proposal has assumed its best possible form.

Debate the Details

At this point, we come to the final sub-component of the law writing process. We started with an idea. We conducted research on that idea by ourselves, individually, or as part of an entmoot. Then we had an independent observer critique the idea presented, and offer advice until we had refined the proposal to the point that we were prepared to defend it in a debate. In society at large, the most professionally polished individuals for debate are generally lawyers, and their usual forum is the courtroom. Historically, trials have evolved from supposed guilt to the presumed innocence of a person, business, or governmental entity. As the adage goes, "innocent until proven guilty." The type of trial that we now propose is a trial of ideas, and it takes place between the individual or entmoot who developed the proposal, the district attorney, and twelve jurors selected at random from the community.[49] This final element we term *causa enim novo,* which is Latin for a *case for change,* but the phrase could also be translated as a *cause for invention*.

The prosecutor, in this respect, is not a sage but rather acts as an opponent of the idea presented. The prosecutor will have access to all the recommendations of the sages but may also call on cosponsors those who may have left the entmoot. He may do this to get an insider perspective on the proposal's issues. As the jurors listen to the pros and cons of the proposal as presented, hopefully, they will be able to uncover the details behind and underneath the proposal that might be missed by voters on election day. After both sides have made the closing arguments, they may discuss the proposal privately among themselves. They each cast an independent vote, either for or against the proposal as submitted. If each vote of a jury member represents a specific number of signatures required to have a proposal placed on the ballot, then each vote will be of some importance to the individual or entmoot submitting the proposal.

---

[49] Trial by Jury, <importanceofphilosophy.com/Politics_TrialByJury.html>.

This does several things. First, because the jury members are made up of residences of that city or locale, it offers a preview of how the city or locale might vote. Second, it is often said of legislation that the *devil is in the details.* The lawyer's job is to identify these possible corrupt intentions, ambiguities, or unintended consequences that may be somewhere in these proposals they are prosecuting and bring those possible objections to the jury's attention. Because these hearings are on the public record, the media and any opposing party have a source available to study for any possible issues should the proposal finally make it onto the ballot. The number of signatures required will be multiplied by the number of jurists who vote against the proposal so that while we do not restrict a person from entering the second primary element of the proposal process, which is the gathering of signatures, it may make the signature-gathering process such a large task that it seems more prudent to refine the proposal and resubmit it for trial to get a more favorable outcome. Of course, the trial results must not be taken lightly. If so, then that individual or entmoot will only consider going to trial after considerable thought has been invested in the proposal's creation. To accomplish this, we stipulate that the individual or entmoot will not be able to resubmit his/her/their proposal for trial for at least one full year. Again, so that a bad proposal may not continue to proceed through the courts year after year, and indefinitely after the same proposal has had three trials, a fourth trial will be granted only if changes or alterations have been made according to the process through the court of appeals.

Step 2: The Prioritizing of Proposals

As we conclude the first element of the law-creation process, the writing and developing of proposals, we move on to the second, which, as you may recall, is prioritizing what is placed on the ballot. We know that there are limits to how many proposals any society can effectively study all at once. If there is only one item on the ballot, naturally it will get maximum scrutiny, and the more proposals there are, the less attention and study each proposal will get. Imagine what would happen if there were fifty proposals on the ballot: Each one would get merely a glance, if that, from the individual voter. With the present system, to limit the number of proposals on the ballot, the state will require signatures from a specified number of persons before the proposal can make it onto the ballot. Getting a person to sign a proposal making it a proposition on the ballot requires a certain type of temperament. People who are naturally outgoing, with a friendly, social disposition, can attract and persuade people to join a cause. This is a valuable skill that may be utilized well in a democratic society, and it is amenable to democratic processes, yet we must also know not all people are so charming. In fact, some of our most brilliant minds have been reclusive introverts. To be fully effective, with the most expressive citizens, democratic societies must find the ways and means for all its concerned citizens—that is, those who chose to participate politically—to express their opinions in ways that will be heard and understood; otherwise, as a democracy that society fails.

The signature-gathering process, as it is, has a second real challenge. The ability to sign proposals that may be placed on the ballot is a requirement for any attempt to achieve direct-democracy because the right to this process allows the people to determine which proposals will go onto the ballots. However, the present system provides no common forum for individuals, for them to see proposals for which members of their community are now soliciting, to obtain the required number of signatures. In the mid-1990s, individuals proposed what they believed was a solution to this with what they referred to as Internet Democracy.

The primary challenge with Internet Democracy—at least with the proposals that I personally have seen—is that it carries with it all the challenges passed down from the democracies of old. Proposals are discussed in chat rooms and then held on a daily or weekly vote, but since anyone may make any proposal or any number of proposals, we see the same rash, ill-advised decision-making processes that plagued the early democracies all over again. Also, anyone who does not stay online *all the time* may miss hundreds, if not thousands, of proposals, and this is, of course, far more than most people could possibly look over, much less study carefully. Also, when one imagines hundreds of proposals *going downstream* every day, like so much *water under the bridge*, it becomes easy to understand why the life and vital energy of this kind of government usually turns out to be dynamic, volatile, and short-lived. The Internet Democracy world also takes it for granted that *everyone who is anyone* has a computer and knows how to use it, and this means that some are automatically excluded for technological reasons. Again, we learn this lesson: Having technology does not mean that people will know how to use it wisely, or to maximum effect. However, we have new possibilities, for the current technology does provide a venue for anyone with a PC, Apple, and Internet-access to participate, and we have seen already, over the past decade, how computer use has in many ways widely enhanced innovative, collaborative group work. The challenge is not the Internet, the hardware, or even the software, but how the new technologies will be used.

In the first element, the writing of proposals, we set about to find and establish ways to amplify the effectiveness of the way the proposals are constructed before being sent to the public. In so doing, we limit the number of proposals in circulation while not limiting anyone truly committed to the law-creation process. At the end of the process, we left the signature requirement to a jury of twelve individuals. Using the jury option also allows for winnowing out proposals with merit that show promise and will most likely be community supported. Using the Internet, it is possible to let the public submit their signature to any proposal that received a tie or majority vote from the *causa enim novo* trial. Remember, this is different from the final voting, which is the last element (we have yet to discuss). Effectively through this online forum, any person can look at the proposals that are available in his or her community and then place a signature next to the ones that person wants to see on the ballot. There is no need to be online all the time, but this method has the same strengths of the Internet in that one may look at the proposals available and submit one's signature to the best-looking proposals. Thus, a democratic system of government comes right into your life, where you live. It is *chez vous*. In some small but significant way, it also puts the responsibility of government into the hands of each person but without the feeling of being compelled to stay online all the time to participate. Beyond that, it provides each one and anyone with the ability to review, study, and research each proposal, according to the need as they decide, at their leisure, feet up, relaxed, in the comfort of their own home. Finally, there is something else this method does as well. For those who happen to be shy or introverted, they have an easy, painless way to submit their own proposal, if it received a majority vote from a jury of their peers. Then their idea will be placed online, and they can let the idea speak for itself.

This site, which we affectionately dub the Willow Wisp, if successful, would be the first Internet democracy ever, with real power and authority available to empower the people through the Web. The willow wisp is a plant, to the world a weed to be pulled, yet according to childhood myth if you make a wish and blow your wish may come true. As you blow the individual wisps spread across the sky in hopes that some of your wisps, dreams, will take root and grow. By placing proposals online, one can see which ballot measures are attempting to become proposals. In the present system, this is done through paid signature gathers, but instead of having proposals by rich who can afford signature gathers outside of the local grocery store or mall when the public does not truly have the time to investigate the proposal at hand and is viewing only the one proposal of the signature gatherer, the public can see all proposals circulating at one location during a time of their choosing and convenience. This present availability is not only on a state-level but nationally and perhaps internationally as well. The united states constitution, as well as numerous nations around the globe, allow their constitution to be changed through amendments to it. The amendment process allows for the majority of states with passed proposals to alter the Constitution, therefore as most states allow for the proposals on the ballot, putting the proposal on the website in numerous nations, each in accordance with the rules and regulations of each specific nation and state allows the people to take back their system of government, whether it is the dreams as laid out in this document or another, it is an idea whose time has come. Now I realize that what I am asking is a great deal of work, but one considers that Lenox is an operating system built by volunteers, this is an option that is not dependent upon politician to put through, but available to all who are willing to put forth the effort required.

Institutions of Learning

The financial responsibilities of the national government are divided among several departments which I have dubbed realms. Among these realms is the educational realm, Willow Wisp, referenced earlier. All libraries, universities, sages, courts related to the passage of proposals, related websites, constitutional quandaries, as well as the vote itself all reside within the Willow Wisp realm. The purpose of this realm is to not only educate the population, but also something more. From Vietnam to the genocide in Gaza, each time the national government breached its constitutional boundaries the students and faculty were among the first to take a stand. There Is a natural bond between the education of society and true societal advancement. This book is proof that advancement is not only technological in nature, but also philosophical, political, and religious. Thus, it seems only fitting the Willow Wisp, the educational halo of Jezreel also be the primary defender of the voice of the cast aside.

To understand the natural bond between democracy and education consider there are people that do not have access to the Internet. Perhaps they are poor and unable to afford a computer, or they are elderly, and the Internet seems too complicated. For a democracy to function at the local level, we need a public institution, free of charge, available for study, learning, and instruction. Fortunately for us, society has evolved such an institution, and you may know that institution as the public library. Libraries in a true democracy serve several vital purposes. They are free to the public, most have Internet-access, and they provide an atmosphere of learning and study not only for those doing research on the proposals that are circulating but also for those who wish to develop their own proposal. For those who have questions, such as: "How do I print out a proposal?" "How can I cast my signature for a proposal?" or, "How can I take part in my government?" a librarian will be there to assist so that the democratic process can truly be available to everyone.

The question comes to mind, which law-creation process, the republic, or direct-democracy, would best utilize the human mind and human potential in general? The founding idea behind the republic was that individual neutral representatives would listen to arguments before any proposed piece of legislation and then cast their vote. The problem with this elementary method of looking at Congress is that it fails to consider the political party structure, such that members of Congress receiving their funding from the party structure, voting in opposition to party carries with it many difficult consequences, and also many congressional representatives have established party-line logic on the issues before even running for office. When considering our congressional officials, it is important to ask, "Are they really listening?" If they have already made up their minds on all the issues presented (which, incidentally, most usually have), debate is futile, and the evolution of the republic is doomed. Let us take an optimistic approach and assume that prior to voting, each congressperson remains open-minded, and is going to Congress to weigh the arguments and cast his or her vote in the public interest. As an institution of learning, Congress is limited to the circumference of the ideas presented on the floor by the various individual speakers. It should also be noted that a congressperson is unable to choose which speakers he or she will hear. Voting takes place frequently, often leaving little time carefully to scrutinize each idea and then weigh them against each other. When votes take place before the Congress, the legislators are unlimited in the kinds of bills brought forward, so that yesterday may be health care and tomorrow could be the environment. These factors make it difficult to learn through the congressional setting. This is simply because Congress was not developed as an institution of learning, but rather as an instrument of the lawmaking process. Congress does, however, provide a forum for debate, which is critical for the law-creation process to occur effectively, and therefore the *causa enim novo* was developed. However, because the jury members are selected randomly from people living in the local population, they do not trade votes or have the pressures or strings of party politics, which means that they can function effectively as neutral observers before casting their vote in the manner intended by the founders of the republic.

Could we truly consider that institutions of learning are an intricate part of the law-creation process in a republic? Libraries and universities were developed historically as institutions of learning. It seems prudent that any democracy, to function, is contingent upon a well-educated, well-informed electorate, where study and information resources are freely available, in a climate of intellectual freedom, where the free exchange of ideas may flourish. To accomplish this environment of learning, it is only natural that the evolution of a free society should begin with the founding and growth of their institutions of learning. The universities, as we discussed previously, have been utilized to analyze proposals, and libraries have been utilized as a public place where the people may learn about the law-creation process and participate in their government, whether it be through sponsoring a proposal or submitting one's signature to a proposal that is found to be agreeable.

I have often heard the question, "How can we create an educated society?" The best way to increase the value of knowledge is to make it worth something. Society's evaluation of knowledge and wisdom is determined by the authority people have or may acquire to use the knowledge and wisdom that they gain. By empowering the cast-aside person in society, study becomes fun and an exciting challenge because of the ability to change society themselves brings reason to wisdom and knowledge, with a sense of participation and personal belonging to a larger meaningful purpose. In society, there are two reasons that most people pursue a college education: The first is to earn a living for themselves and the family they have or for which they hope, and the second is for personal development, as a hobby, or to enjoy a dream, as an aspiration—to achieve self-realization. The best circumstances are when the two reasons can become one and the same, although unfortunately, that is not always the case. The striking difference between these two methods is that one is learning through obligation, and the other is learning through desire. If you remember back to your days in school, which method of learning did you prefer? In Congress, voting takes place often on a variety of subjects, which means that the members have an obligation to research bills and proposals that do not pique the representatives' core wants and desires. In a direct-democracy, on the other hand, when submitting his or her signature to a proposal, the signer is free to choose and study just the issues that appeal to those core, personal, heartfelt desires. Ultimately, the goal is to let each person follow one's own calling, perfecting that social concern, and collectively working to improve the whole society and the whole planet.

As you must have noticed already, when you read here about creating laws, we always refer to *creating laws within the community*. Yet we need ways of tying these independent communities together. All nations do this through many ways, such as through public acts and records. For example, birth, marriage, death certificates from one community in the nation are shared and honored by the rest of the nation as are college degrees, criminal histories, etc., etc. Yet we must also provide ways for allowing the law to be expanded beyond these bounds, such as over a whole state, or nationwide. We have developed two ways to accomplish this. The first is to make it easier for a community to place a proposal on the ballot after another community has passed it. Since the process we laid out here for the creation of law has already been established once a proposal has been passed by the vote, there is no need to go through the exact same lengthy requirements elsewhere to place the same proposal on the ballot. By allowing other communities to acquire the proposals for circulation among a pool of proposals that have passed with only a small fraction of the number of required signatures each person in society will then have much more proposals from which to choose. Teamwork and cooperation between the communities may assist in the entire process of understanding new proposals, appropriately modifying existing ones, and better implementing already-existing laws.

Creating Movements

The question naturally arises; how long will a person have for the gathering of signatures? In the present proposition system in the United States, a person is granted one election cycle in which to gather all the signatures required after the proposal has been submitted initially to the government entity. This has several issues about it because corporations and other large organizations have built-in structures to gather the signatures they need, but for the cast-aside person, this turns out to be an obstacle course with tough sledding. A person could knock himself out and still obtain only about three-quarters of the signatures needed. With the new system I propose, I seek to make it as easy as possible for those who can argue successfully in court. Still, the requisite number of signatures may still be a troublesome obstacle, especially in communities with larger populations, such as Cairo, Istanbul, or Jerusalem. It is also to be hoped that people will study the available proposals seriously before they sign their names indicating their approval. Therefore, the process of having a person submit his or her signature to a proposal was done through the Internet and libraries because these institutions were developed for research and discovery. Nevertheless, the full process of research and discovery, if true and effective, takes time. On the other hand, technology is always moving ahead, and the possibility remains that if a proposal does not make it onto the ballot if enough people in society realize its need, another proposal will come along later and fill that void. Therefore, it will often happen that proposals that may have seemed perfect originally with the passage of time will become outdated or even completely obsolete. The universe, in its constant, upward drive for improvement, periodically raises the ante, so that what was once considered completely adequate and wonderful by one and all has a way of becoming outmoded or even a nuisance. To address these concerns, every twenty years, the proposals that never completed the signature process—if they are were done more than five years previously—will be dismissed. Therefore, at a minimum, all people will have at least five years to get the number of signatures they need for their proposal to be placed on the ballot and at the same time, as conditions change, remain current. In addition, no proposal without enough signatures may stay on the books for more than twenty-five years. Each day fads change. What is popular one day is obsolete the next. It is expected that some proposals will rise and fall with the times and seasons, but others will slowly grow strong over time. This system and the democracy itself are limited to the power and abilities of the people. Its strengths originate in the strengths of humankind and also its weaknesses.

In the present system, as you may know, the number of signatures required determines the priority of the initiatives to be placed on the ballot. The greater the population, the more signatures are required. Because of this rule, in the present system the authorization to put a proposal on the local ballot requires only a few signatures, and therefore it remains somewhat available to the cast-aside person, but because the power structure of republics start at the top and flow down, there are few items that a person may alter at even the city level, because the powers granted to cities are comparatively few. But to place proposals on the ballot on the shire level, more powers are available to those wishing to create or change laws, yet it is more difficult for the cast-aside person because the number of signatures required to place a proposal on that ballot is also greater. This continues up to the state-level, where even greater powers are available for those who wish to create proposals, yet the number of signatures is so excessive that only corporations or wealthy, influential persons can obtain the number of required signatures. Constantly and incrementally adding to these difficulties, the world's population is expanding, and the required number of signatures will continue to expand to the point that a person's ability to place a proposal on the ballot will become next to—if not actually in all cases—impossible. In fact, in most republics today, there are no propositions being placed on the national ballot, and legislators operating at the national level (Senators and Representatives in Congress in the U.S.) seem to feel that such popular measures could diminish their personal power, though few would admit to this. Even if they did so agree, the number of signatures required would be so astronomically great that the typical person would have difficulty imagining getting involved. For a democracy to function, unlike a republic, the people themselves must be the actual power base. This also means that the power must start at the bottom, as a foundation, and work its way upward. Therefore, the more powers that are available at, the lower levels of government, the more the cast-aside person is empowered and will take responsibility for passing the propositions that, in turn, become the laws that will govern the whole society.

As we brought up previously in the republic the party system is looking for people who will be subservient to the parties wishes, leaving behind their own ideas, never venturing outside of the box. Thus, those in congress being subservient to their donors are not truly there for their own ideas, but to advance their political power. As all new ideas are transformed to short stereotypical labels a seat in congress becomes less about cause and more about the power and prestige of the office. However, in a direct democracy the sponsors are unelected, and thus unpaid citizens of the nation. The cause is championed over a seat in a position of power, as it is in a republic. As a proposal begins to move from community to community, the person who wrote the law originally will be there to promote the cause that inspired the proposal in the first place. Depending on the success of the proposal, throughout the communities, the sponsors will come to be recognized as people fighting for that cause or purpose. Think about those you admire most: Washington, Lincoln, Gandhi, Martin Luther King Jr., or Nelson Mandela, to name a few. The remarkable thing about these people is that they cared little for themselves, their lives were devoted to a socially meaningful cause. They were truly helpful while at the same time, they were way-showers to their followers. On the other extreme, we see history's worst villains: Hitler, Stalin, and much more, all of whom, in one way or another, seem to have been regularly obsessed with their own standing and their own reputation than with the needs of their people. Thus, our goal in leadership is to naturally draw out people from within society with the right heart for the job. Jesus taught: *The greatest among you will be your servant. For whoever exalts himself will be humbled, and he who humbles himself will be exalted*[50], and Ali said... *Never say to yourself, 'I am their Lord, their ruler...and I must be obeyed submissively and humbly. Such a thought will unbalance your mind, will make you vain and arrogant, will weaken your faith in religion and will make you seek the support of any power other than God's...*[51]

One of the major challenges with a Republican form of government is that one votes *for people* rather than for propositions, programs, or strategic plans. A person may say many things, but politicians do not freely reveal their dark sides. Appearances may be deceiving, and cunning politicians who lack wisdom and who are running for office may fool the electorate. Unfortunately, there always seem to be some with devious plans, intentions, or paybacks to be given, and the laws they manage to get passed or the favors they bestow may have a way of suddenly revealing their dark side only after Election Day. Our attempt to design a direct-democracy style of government represents an attempt to create a society that is solidly based on a foundation of ideas rather than of people—a government of laws rather than of men, as the adage goes. The great payoff here should be that in a society based on ideas, people who are cause-based and supporting socially meaningful causes rather than those who are out to amplify themselves only can begin to emerge. As sponsors obtain more signatures movements are formed and grow with time. Thus, the law creation process catapults cause based people into the public spotlight and out of those people will come your mayors, judges, and societal leadership in a direct democracy, because unlike a republic the idea champions the citizen, rather than the seat they hold. Beyond that we can be certain these candidates will enforce the law in word and spirit because they wrote it. And thus, society is created by those that stick their neck out, rather than the cowards in congress who fear the loss of their power over the need in society.

Step 3: Passage of Proposals into Law

Further analyzing local law in relation to the national law allows us to move onto the final step in the law-creation process, the actual passage of propositions. Society's closest expression of this final element in the law-creation process is the vote. Even the vote itself can add to the level of tyranny over one's ideas because those who were not in the majority finish by being on the losing side of a vote. For example, a nation has a vote whether Proposition A should become law. One-hundred sixty million people vote for it, and a hundred and forty million people vote against it. With the majority vote, Proposition A becomes law. One-hundred sixty million people were represented, but for a hundred and forty million people, the law was contrary to their wishes, and in those terms, their voices as individuals were suppressed. Now we go deeper into our analysis of the vote, and we discover that the states of Utah, New Mexico, and Florida all had majorities in opposition to Proposition A, so let us say we pass Proposition A just in the States wherein a majority of people voted in favor. Now we have, let us say, two hundred million individuals represented, but there are still a

---

[50] Levi 23:11–12.

[51] Qur'an quotes and references logic, <religiousconsultation.org /hassan2.htm>; * Quran 17: 70, 33:72, 2:30–34, 42:21.

hundred million people who were not represented. Next, we go down to the shire (county) level (or, as counties are variously denominated in a few northeastern states, townships). Only in those shires where the Proposition passed will it become law. Now there are two hundred and seventy-five million people who are represented, and a mere twenty-five million people who are not. Thus, as it turns out, shires are a much more essential aspect of democracy than most people realize.

When the United States as a nation was formed, the states were not solid boundaries, as they exist today. Off to the west, there were territories, mostly inhabited by Indians, fur traders, and poor families searching for land. In the east, there were border disputes between New Hampshire and New York. Since travel was much more difficult than it is today, most states had relatively little landmass, such as Maryland, Rhode Island, and Delaware, which were among the smallest. It was also not uncommon in those days for a state to divide itself, thus allowing its inhabitants to feel better represented by their state government. For instance, Vermont was once claimed by New York, Kentucky and West Virginia were once parts of Virginia, and Maine once belonged to Massachusetts. It is doubtful the designers of the American Constitution could have imagined states the size of California that rivaled the landmass and diversity of all thirteen original colonies, or Texas, or the largest of them all, Alaska. These larger states—California, Oregon, Washington, Texas, and Idaho, to name a few, each has significant internal divisions with major, different competing interests within themselves. To assist the state governments in managing their internal affairs, the states were subdivided into individual shires.

If each shire could govern itself, would the people living there feel better represented by their government? To answer this question, let us look now, for instance, at California, the state in which I was born. If California were subdivided into its individual counties (shires), would the people living there feel better represented? The middle counties (shires) are located between San Francisco and Los Angeles, which are made up mostly of rural farmers. Farmers who, because of their small towns' populations, sometimes feel that they have scant representation in the state legislature even though these same Californian Farmers represent the largest agricultural center in the nation. The southeastern counties (shires) are made up of large desert communities and Indian tribes that feel oppressed by the state and have many concerns and issues about water rights and the international border with Mexico and illegal immigration. The northern counties (shires) are mostly conservative, with rural, agricultural, and forested land, and they identify with the counties (shires) in southern Oregon, unlike the people in the lower two-thirds of California. Finally, there are the three highly populated counties (shires) next to the Pacific Ocean, including Los Angeles County, Orange County, and San Francisco. These three counties (shires) represent over sixty percent of the state's population and therefore dominate the interests of the state legislature. Also, it is not surprising that the people who live there, in those three counties (shires), do not have much of a clue that people in the rest of the state feel underrepresented and disenfranchised—because of them. Moreover, as I traveled about elsewhere in the United States, I discovered this same political tension elsewhere. For instance, people in southern Oregon seem to feel that because the Eugene/Portland/Willamette Valley area has three-quarters of the state's population and is growing much faster in population than the rest of the state, then their wants and needs must be too often overlooked or summarily passed over in the state's overall scheme of things. For these obvious reasons, then, I reached the conclusion that the more localized the representation could be put into place, the more well represented each person would feel. Thomas Jefferson referred to the powers of local representation this way: *The extent of our country was so great, and its former division into distinct States so established, that we thought it better to confederate as to foreign affairs only. Every state retained its self-government in domestic matters, as better qualified to direct them to the good and satisfaction of their citizens, than a general government so distant from its remoter citizens and so little familiar with the local peculiarities of the different parts.*[52]

But then, how far down can this obvious thinking go? Consider the townships in the eastern United States. They are often infinitely smaller than the smallest counties in California. For instance, Loving County, Texas has a population of 94 and Swains Island County, Samoa has a population of 17. Each shire needs enough citizens to be financially solvent as well as enough combinations of cities, towns, and\or villages to form a Shire Fellowship. In a general practice this means that the more densely populated the region the smaller the land mass that is needed to constitute a shire. For instance, in New York City a shire may have a landmass of a mile, while places like Alaska a shire may cover hundreds of miles. The smaller the group of people there is, the less able that group is to maintain the normal local government functions, with courts, police, schools, medical care, etc., until it cannot function properly as such. This is why, possibly, and in my opinion, the county (shire) system is the smallest existing governmental system that can effectively enforce the law. The county (shire) system for the western states: California, Oregon, Washington, etc. (not coincidentally) is the most similar governmental system relative to the size and population of the original thirteen American colonies, for which the American Constitution was established.

If we go down one level from there, and divide the nation into cities, say, only those cities where Proposition A passed, we have a major challenge because there are large land areas that are not under the jurisdiction of any city, whereas all people, apart from sailors, reside within a shire. In addition, for laws to be supported, there must be some body of governance, such as a mayor, a police force, and a court infrastructure to enforce the laws.

The Foundational Elements of Democracy

However, there is another, smaller but still vitally important foundation for any democratic society. The family unit has functioned effectively generation after generation for the optimal well-being of children, even when and where there were no governments. While people make mistakes and abuses do occur, the family, as a social structure remains, overall, highly effective. Therefore Article 16 (3) of the U.N.

---

[52] In Defense of Democracy - <etext.virginia.edu/jefferson/quotations/>, Letter to William Stevens Smith (November 13, 1787), quoted in Padover's *Jefferson on Democracy*, <en.wikiquote.org/wiki/Thomas_Jefferson>.

Universal Declaration of Human Rights establishes protection for the family unit, "The family is the natural and fundamental group unit of society and is entitled to protection by society and the State.[53]"

Any democratic government that, to any great degree imposes its will on how a family should raise its children is threatening society's greatest source of stability. This is because it is through their parents that children learn social behavior. Let us use an example for easier comprehension the creation of laws at the community level, and a certain community decides that a child who lives there should be able to smoke tobacco products or drink alcoholic beverages at the age of sixteen. However, a parent may not want his or her child to smoke or drink ever. As you will recall, previously, we mentioned that social maturity is a relative matter for each individual person. When a child has left his parents' home and has been living independently, as specified in the law, that person is legally now an adult, with limitations on his or her behavior only to the same extent as other citizens who must also obey the laws, rather than also the behavioral boundaries imposed by parents. Yet until that child moves out of the parents' home, the parents take on most legal responsibilities of that child. While the child is living under the parents' roof the parents, rather than society, should have the power to determine when a child is old enough to participate in specific activities, such as viewing certain kinds of movies, wearing certain kinds of clothes, or which friends may come to visit at the parents' home. If a society is prepared to dictate to all parents how a child should be raised, then society is to a certain extent making the state accountable for child-rearing, and thereby voiding the parents' natural responsibilities. This would be a huge loss of liberty and responsibility for any caring parent. Parents, unlike society, have the benefit of seeing and working with their children every day. Society will never be able to put the time and love that most parents naturally put into the raising of their children, nor are the courts particularly skillful at resolving domestic issues about children, such as custody disputes. In fact, many serious errors occur. For these reasons, then, parental and other natural family rights, and the specific rights of the family unit over that of society must be preserved.

The problem in our existing legal structure is that all laws are setup from the standpoint of society, from the legal age for drinking, viewing movies, and other rights rather than from the standpoint of parental rights. For example, in Jewish homes, it has been commonplace for the last millennium for children to have a small glass of wine with their meal. The problem in the present system is that the constitution and bill of rights were designed around the needs of individual liberty, yet there are no amendments to the Constitution to express rights parents do have regarding their children.

On the other hand, we also know that while most parents do at least a tolerable job of raising their children, many do not. At one extreme, there are parents who beat their children, and on the other, there are children who are rarely disciplined or managed properly, as becomes apparent when discipline issues arise at daycare facilities, or at school. Society also may not ignore these issues, because each child

---

[53] UN 1948 Universal Declaration of Human Rights, <un.org/Overview/rights.html>.

so improperly raised will carry these challenges into adulthood, when the rights of others will be encroached upon, to the detriment and expense of society. There are two different issues here, and each one requires a different means to deal with its own unique conditions. Those parents found to have beaten or molested their child should be dealt with through the law. Depending on the degree of the offense, their past history, the opinions of social workers, and other experts the courts may consult, and other relevant circumstances, since they have been irresponsible parents, they may forfeit their natural rights to raise the child, who may become the ward of the state.

When we look at the second extreme, if a child becomes an extreme discipline challenge at school, it is likely that the parents are also having disciplinary issues with the child at home. Often times, professional counseling by psychologists or clergy are needed to help parents understand better how to fulfill their parenting duties. By any account, the raising of children is a huge responsibility, no two children are alike, and unique or unusual circumstances may apply. When any person chooses to become a parent, except by rape, they must be considered as having willingly accepted the responsibilities of the raising of children, and of doing it properly.

I believe it is important to establish a difference between beating a child and spanking a child. Parents have different methods to discipline their children, and these matters always require good judgment and should not involve any abuses of their authority. There are many parents who are good people and who spank their child in a manner that a social worker would not consider abusive to that child. Sadly, many of these good parents also live with the fear that people may see or find out about such brief incidents, and then they may have the child taken away. This is the same general fear that we spoke about earlier, that a society may come to dictate how a parent should raise his or her children. Tyranny is the use of law to hinder a person from performing some act the person believes is natural, right, and justified. We would not want many people to live in fear that if using measures they see as reasonable and justified to discipline their child, then the state could take away the child. Many psychologists have the opinion that spanking a child is not usually the best way to discipline, and our purpose is not to dispute that expert opinion, but it is also true that spanking is a traditional method of discipline embedded in many cultures around the world. Of course, all children are different, and what works with one may not work with another, but there are also parents who abuse their authority. For this reason, our Constitution distinguishes spanking from beating so as not to infringe needlessly upon the rights of parents. In most circumstances, a parent—even if that parent is not the best—will be a much better parent to the child than the state. Jezreel, we should remember, is not about amplifying the rights of the majority, but about amplifying the rights of every person. By putting the rights of the family unit above the powers granted to society at large to dictate its right over its members, we conclude by amplifying the individual person's rights.

Among the strengths of the family is that the parents, not the state unveil the world to their children. In American schools, even elementary schools, the parent is not allowed to enter the facility or monitor the classroom, nor allow video. During the COVID epidemic when children were sent home to learn remotely the parents had a wake-up call. Reading, writing, and arithmetic had taken a backseat to social reengineering. However, social re-engineering is not purely reserved for the young, but also used to re-engineer society through the use of propaganda. Propaganda occurs when the government has control over the nation's media. Among the most infamous abuses of this was Joseph Goebbels who worked directly with Hitler to control the German press. This brings us to the free speech dilemma. On one hand you have nations that opening propagandize their people such as the Soviet Union and Communist China. But on the other hand, the so-called *free nations* of the world also covertly propagandize not only their own people but also greater humanity. Recently it was discovered the United States was paying Politico, the New York Times, and multiple other news sources through the public coffers from the US Agency for International Development (USAID) as propaganda machines for their benefit. In case any should doubt the motivations of USAID, it should be noted that their covert propaganda machine was responsible for toppling the legitimately elected governments of Ukraine, Iran, Chile, and Egypt, among others. Among the propaganda was to censor the genocide of the people of Gaza in which over half a million people were murdered. The FBI and other government agency also went to media outlets so that Google and Meta also censored the public. And foreign news outlets, such as TikTok that they couldn't censor were banned outright. Ironically whistleblowers such as CIA leak Edward Snowden and Wiki Leaks founder Julian Assange were made examples of US prosecution for their speech, not for lying, but for telling the American people the truth. The dilemma comes with how to you deal with the problem. The freedom of speech is so vital that societies know that any rules on it will be abused by those in positions of power. Yet to create no laws allows the government to cover up the worst of offenses, even and including genocide, with immunity from prosecution. The United States Republic is built upon a separation of powers: executive, judicial, and legislative. Yet there remains a fourth branch, not of the government, but of the people that must remain separated from all government entanglements and that branch is the free press. I can make laws restricting government employees from interfering with the press. I can establish laws that restrict taxpayer resources to covertly fund any press agency that may create the appearance of impropriety. I can require full disclosure of all funds between the government and any press entity. I can extend freedom of speech to include foreign press agencies and noncitizens, so that whether in war or peace, speech, assembly, and the press remain a right for all humanity. But the problem still remains because every law is dependent on those in power to implement. Propaganda is a tool of the powerful who all too frequently manipulate the law to work for their advantage. Therefore, the weapon against propaganda must come from the people. The prophets recognized this only to well. For the sake of truth Jeremiah was thrown in a well, Isaiah was sawed in two, John the Baptist was beheaded, and Jesus inherited the cross. So the question is how do I create a system that amplifies and empowers the voice of the little man. Not just to create law, but to be able to stand in opposition to the power of the state and retain their voice when the powerful wish to muzzle it? To answer this, I must embed in the fabric of the system methods to unravel the strength of the powerful, which is fame and money.

The business world through capitalism is run to make a profit, whereas the religious world through moralism is run to bring good to the world. Each of us have a choice of two paths. You can walk the path of fame, fortune, and domination. Or you can walk the path of truth and justice. A person can walk either path, but they can't walk both. As Christ said you can't serve two masters, either you will serve God or money. To choose a profession as a journalist has a religious element to it. At its core is the fight for truth and justice. Yet today media giants own hundreds of different press agencies. When the public hears multiple sources, which they perceive to be independent, all saying the same thing it gives the impression of credible sources, yet this deception is intentional. When the press follows the path of money they take society with them on the road to hell. The editors are responsible for determining which articles are published. Therefore, it is essential to have rules in place to ensure that the editors are neither controlled by government nor the media's wealthy overlords. That the press truly remains under a separation of powers as it were. To maintain this, I stipulate that press organizations must be employee-owned, in that each employee has an equal share of the organization and the editors elected annually by the employees through an anonymous vote. Beyond that if a media conglomerate owns several subagencies, each vote is to be independent within the employees of each subsidiary. Anonymous surveys are also to be taken to see if journalist believe they can be truly objective or if stories that go against public opinion are suppressed. The results of these surveys are to be made public. If voter rights or anonymity is questioned the Willow Wisp courts are there. If the rights of labor are abused the Fruit of the Spirit realm courts are there. In this way, each element of the press is as its own independent little democracy, neither under the umbrella of the government nor controlled by the private sector, but separate and free.

The Fruit of the Spirit realm is designed to ensure the rights of the little man. When the ship runs a ground, it is important to note who is manning the oar. I have worked for many corporations. At one corporation after being ignored by management for months I went to the ombudsman's office to report against the actions of management. GE required each employee to sign a nondisclosure agreement. After visiting the ombudsman's office one of their lawyers contacted me who demanded I perjure myself, stating, *if you reveal what is going on here in court you would be violating the nondisclosure agreement, and we will sue you and you could lose your house!* Everything I told them was ignored and in the end the Garden Grove, CA, Boca Raton, FL and Tualatin, OR branches were closed. Hundreds of innocent people lost their jobs through the arrogance of management who were too important to listen to the complaints of the little people on the bottom. This is not to argue against capitalist competition, but to point out that when poorly run organizations go under those who pay the price for failure are often blameless because they were provided no voice in the decisions of management. Beyond that my mother was a teacher and my father was an auditor for Los Angeles County. Each night around the dinner table they would complain about the corruption of management in their respective fields.

Thus, corruption is everywhere, because as human beings we each have a road to walk either toward God or money.

Among the greatest difficulties for any journalist is finding legitimate sources at the bottom who are willing to put everything on the line to inform the people on what is going on in their government and business enterprises. The Fruit of the Spirit realm is designed to be a liaison between the whistleblower and the press, such that the Fruit of the Spirit can investigate the allegations of the whistleblower and then be the source for the press so that the whistleblower maintains anonymity. This is not to say businesses don't have rights. Contracts, copyrights, license agreements, etc. are enforced by the Oz realm which we will discuss later. However, it is important to maintain a separation of powers so that those responsible for enforcing the rights of private enterprise are different than those who maintain the rights of labor. Beyond that how these rights are enforced are thus also different. The Fruit of the Spirit realm goes beyond labor to investigate the causes of poverty in all forms and seek out remedy. As the good book says helping the poor is lending to God and he pays back with interest.[54]

It would be best if all law were local to reflect the needs of the family, organization, or local community, but there is still a need for national law to ensure the fundamental rights overriding rights humanity are enforced. There are also other kinds of laws that must remain national, such as those governing military matters, immigration, and trade. As history has proven, there are many ways in which national law may be developed. Yet with a world that now has billions of people, how can laws be created that reflect accurately the real desires and wishes of all the people? Secondly, how, in the face of national law, are the powers of the local community to be maintained?

It is vital to understand that any attempt to improve government starts with the fundamental appreciation for the so-called *ordinary person* or the *cast-aside man*. Not only that, but one must learn how to appreciate the ordinary person in the fields or on the streets as the strength of government rather than its weakness. With this book, to continue the positive, progressive evolution of government is not the point. We can say, *myth or illusion*, that people will never accept change. We could say that what we now attempt and conceptually design will never, in fact, be implemented. On the other hand, we can challenge the status quo and stand with the few never-say-die human spirits that have always struggled with the greatest perseverance against all odds, no matter what the obstacles came against them.[55] The point is that one day the government of this world will evolve, with or without our help. This is true because of several of the most basic facts about human-beings. Humans, from the time of their birth, have an inherent dislike for any limitations on their liberty. Our species also benefits—in emotional and psychological terms—by identifying with and taking a stand for, what a person believes is right, no matter what the risks might be, and even though there may be no tangible or obvious reward. We have intelligent energies, intuitively we understand our sources of power, and we are averse to whatever seems to be, in this deep sense, threatening. Finally, we can understand

[54] Proverbs 19:17.

[55] Samuel 17:40–47.

and appreciate these inherent, natural qualities of the human spirit, embedded in our nature, even better, and see them as natural adaptations to our world, if we are also prepared to think of reality itself as open-ended.

Committees

Historically governments have never relinquished their powers to the people without a rebellion of one form or another. The republic evolved out of the monarchy to allow the people a way to redress their grievances. Its invention and framework are spelled out in the book *the Republic* by the philosopher Plato. Romulus commissioned the first Senate with a hundred Senators for a population perhaps as high as 35,000 and the Roman Republic was born. In time the Roman Empire would expand to 75 million inhabitants, though only male roman citizens were allowed to vote and as the population grew the number of seats in the Senate grew as well, until the Senate was no longer an effective counterbalance to the demigod Caesar as the Roman Republic transitioned to the Roman Empire. There reaches a point in population growth where either a parliament has too many representatives for any individual representative to have a meaningful voice or where each member is representing such a vast number of people that the voice of each citizen becomes completely lost. For instance, while India's Rajya Sabha (Parliament) is limited to no more than 250 members, Tamil Nadu has 18 representatives for 72 million inhabitants, Bihar (104 million) and West Bengal (91 million) have 16 representatives. On the reverse side of the equation China has nearly 3000 members in their congress as of 2023. Such numbers are well beyond what Plato architecture intended for the machine. When a nation by instinct compels other nations to follow its form of government, as the United States would like to do with China, these legitimate questions must come up for serious consideration. Consider that if one had a community of three thousand people, would they not say that our community is too large to represent everyone and that there should be a smaller elected body? Among the hopes for world peace is uniting the world through a singular Republic, such as the United Nations, but if individual nations have become too large to provide their people with representation, then a global government of the same model would be infinitely worse. Thus, humanity's failure to evolve past the republic, to Jezreel, is among the greatest impediments to world peace. The republic has no guidelines about how many elected representatives are too few and how many are too many. Possibly what counts about this is the nature of the topic under debate, but the fact remains that these unknown variables present the natural limitations of the republic. Without realistic boundaries in place, societies have expanded the natural limits of the republics well beyond their inherent ability adequately to represent their people. Machine growth of the republic without any evaluation of the cause and effect to representation has accelerated the need for alternative forms of government by using greater and more effective forms of representation. As our goal is the unity of the Arab Nations, a civilization like the stars of the sky and the sand of the seashore, one can see how this can be an issue.

This brings us to one of the greatest questions that face all attempts to establish direct-democracy: "If, with an ever-growing population, Congress provides less and less representation, how can each person in a direct-democracy get more and better representation?" To answer this question, we must turn it around. The people to be served by a government are not the cause of a government's challenges, but rather *they are the solution to the government's challenge*. By retaining the sovereignty and relative independence of the shire governments, the people of that shire do not have to contend politically with the ever-growing national population. If the population becomes too large, to maintain and enhance the representation of the people, the shire may divide along political lines. Jefferson said it this way: *But how collect [the people's] voice? This is the real difficulty. If invited by private authority, [to] county (shire) or district meetings, these divisions are so large that few will attend; and their voice will be imperfectly, or falsely, pronounced. Here, then, would be one of the advantages of the ward divisions I have proposed. The mayor of every ward, on a question like the present, would call his ward together, take the simple yea or nay of its members, convey these to the country court, who would hand on those of all its wards to the proper general authority; and the voice of the whole people would be thus fairly, fully, and peaceably expressed, discussed, and decided by the common reason of the society.*[56]

Since each person is only allowed to submit one proposal (which may be either local or national), we know that local proposals will always be advocated for the simple reason that local government often has been given authority greater than the national government, such as with firearms use and ownership, gambling, drug laws, and penalties for various crimes that have been restricted from the realm law-creation process. This, too, is in line with Jeffersonian principle, for, as he said: *The several States composing the United States of America are not united on the principle of unlimited submission to their General Government; but ... by a compact under the style and title of a Constitution for the United States, and of amendments thereto, they constituted a General Government for special purposes—delegated to that government certain definite powers, reserving, each State to itself, the residuary mass of right to their own self-government.*[57]

Local proposals are also easier to accomplish. At the same time, we realize that on a national level, there are only so many issues of the day that may be considered. We know that there remains a need that we cannot avoid for national law. In a republic one party and thus one philosophical element dominates the majority, but in a direct democracy all philosophical elements are welcome to present one, or even multiple proposals on the same issues. Therefore, if a person wants to submit a national proposal, the first requirement in that process should be to make sure that no-one else has submitted the exact same—or extremely similar—proposal already. This will also create an attraction for group consideration among similar proposals. Remember in a democracy all concepts submitted through proposals belong to the people, thus all proposals are public domain as no copywrite exists. This also means that sponsors of the same subject should learn from the wisdom of one another. Plagiarism should be encouraged allowing the sponsors to take the best of the proposals circulating in the same area of study. The main legislative difference

---

[56] In Defense of Democracy, <etext.virginia.edu/jefferson/quotations/>, Letter to William Stevens Smith (November 13, 1787), quoted in Padover's *Jefferson on Democrac, y*<en.wikiquote.org/wiki/Thomas_Jefferson>.

[57] Ibid.

between the number of proposals circulating in a republic and a direct-democracy is the sheer quantity of proposals. How successful these political structures are will depend largely on how easy it is to find and bring together people behind like-minded proposals, and then for them to work together constructively, with good teamwork. This process of bringing like-minded ideas together has been utilized in the republics, with the development of their committee structures, and that provided members of Congress or Parliament with the ability to form their own committees. In its elementary forms, this process has been seen working well for centuries; in fact, you may recall your days in high school when students gravitated naturally towards their classmates with their same interests, such as sports, music, chess, drama, foreign languages, etc. Therefore, it is important to understand in a historical way the strengths and weaknesses of the advances of government in these areas, which will enable us to maximize their strengths and minimize their inherent weaknesses.

The larger republics become, the more members there should be in their lawmaking agencies. This growth creates the need for internal legislatures within the primary legislature. For example, in the U.S. Congress, one legislature studies Medicare, while another studies Social Security, and yet another military matters. These individual legislatures within legislatures are what we call *committees.* The larger the population, the larger each committee gets, and the more committees and committee members there must be. Before legislation reaches the floor of the Congress, it must pass through the committees. Because of the power they wield, some committees are bound to be more popular than others. Each committee has a head congressperson or senator, who presides and serves as its chair, and that chair is determined by seniority. Therefore, the longer a person has been in Congress, the greater chance that person has to get into an influential committee, or even to chair that committee, such as the powerful House Ways and Means Committee, which by law must introduce all tax legislation to Congress. The chair of that committee is often spoken of as the most powerful person in the House of Representatives after the Speaker. Obviously, this plan strongly favors the most experienced—and often oldest—members of Congress.

This organizational structure of political specialization has several distinct advantages in that it keeps individual members of Congress focused sharply on some particular areas of governmental concern, and at the same time allows the population to continue growing while also retaining some powers of the individual representatives. To our considerable misfortune, however, it also contains several major flaws. First, many persons seek congressional office because they are passionate about a given cause. For instance, a medical doctor may not like certain laws governing the medical community, or a career soldier who goes off to Congress may dislike the hierarchical organizational structure, or certain practices going on in the military services. The insights of these new members of Congress are important because they see and understand what is happening in their respective specialty areas of concern. Because committees and chairs of committees are granted by seniority, and partially depending upon which party holds the majority, our new member of Congress, has little to no chance of getting onto his or her most desired committees, in which there would be relevant expertise based on that person's own personal experience and/or from other special knowledge or training—not to mention heading it. Now it is true that if they can hold out in Congress for a few terms, then finally they may get onto the committee they wanted, and maybe even get lucky enough to have their own party in power when they finally get that position. But as time goes on, the issues and the powers that be within that industry or sector invariably change, however, and by the time the freshman congressperson finally gets into a position to effect productive political change, the person's drive, interests, and determination to effect positive change in that industry or sector may have long since departed, and the once-prized special knowledge may have now become yesterday's news, *old hat*, or worse. By this time, they have become congressional insiders rather than people out there in the real-world, actively engaged in the front lines of the industry. Because of this common development, legislators often need to go back to the industry or that particular sector to ask questions about how things have changed. This, in turn, leads us on to a fundamental challenge in the corporate world. The view from the top is always different from that at or near the bottom, and the underclass people near the bottom may be able to see challenges clearly, but to go against management may seem to mean the loss of a big promotion or even the job. Sometimes people will confide in the after-hours janitor, pouring out their frustrations, more readily than they will make a clean breast of things with their supervisors, and this happens often because the after-hours janitor has no power to implement significant changes, and is safe, with no power to jeopardize anyone's career. So, too, with bartenders, who often know what matters most in the power structures of their own local community. Most regrettably, when a congressional person asks a question of the people of an industry, those people well know that they may risk losing their jobs or a promotion if certain sensitive information is passed along that management would like concealed from the public, and this is true of both for-profit and nonprofit enterprises in the private and public sectors. Key public decisions, therefore, may depend ultimately upon such subtle, tenuous skills of an elected representative as the ability *to read between the lines* or knowing exactly how to get blood out of a turnip in interview processes that turn out to be inherently problematic.

There is also another unavoidable reality that works against the lawmakers of a republic. As technology increases, so goes the pace of change in society itself. Changes in industries that once took decades or even centuries to achieve are now accomplished in years, weeks, or days. It also regularly happens in our free-enterprise system that new technologies are introduced willy-nilly into the marketplace without any serious thought or due consideration given to the legal and moral ramifications of the new technologies. Then, later, when the inevitable social challenges develop because of this lack of organized political foresight, and legislators and government officials are besieged with complaints from their disgruntled or angry constituents, and government agencies then must struggle desperately to *play catch-up*. In relation to technological innovations, an obvious ongoing disjunction between the profit motive that drives the free-enterprise and adequate social planning, with governmental oversight exists.

We can still acknowledge that, to the benefit of the people served by the republic, when the congressperson finally does make it onto the desired committee, the chances are that not *all* the original vital energy towards positive, constructive change has yet been dissipated, not *all* that original knowledge has been rendered by changing circumstances obsolete, and not *all* those original, creative ideas hopelessly outmoded. Yet before they made it onto the coveted committees, which they went originally to Congress to change, there were all the years they spent on the various *ad-hoc* committees and subcommittees upon which they dutifully did their time because those were the slots that were open. Hence, the fact remains that during those years of however long preparation and impatiently getting ready, that Representative or Senator may have had no substantive or important knowledge of that industry but was still nevertheless dutifully casting votes with a direct impact on the lives of millions.

In the new government model, we attempt to form the evolutionary equivalent of committees by narrowing the focus of the kinds of legislation that people may propose. By always limiting our direct democratic participation in legislation to one subject per person, this allows a person to choose the area upon which he or she wants to focus at any one-time, which may be the first-time. This strategy also allows each person to study the industry or service while he or she is employed in that enterprise, which means that the person's judgment and perception may change and *grow along* with the ever-changing technology. By contrast, in a republic each legislator, while being perhaps a member of only one committee, may nonetheless submit an endless number of proposals on a wide variety of subjects. For example, some of the legal matters for which a congressperson on the Health and Human Services Committee is responsible include: proposing new law or laws regarding the Food and Drug Administration, health management organizations, medical insurance, budgetary needs for Medicare and Medicaid, laws about people who lack health insurance, medical malpractice, and how original medical research is done. Then, of course, there are the normal duties all members of Congress have, including running for office, meeting with concerned citizens, giving speeches, attending banquets and formal dinners, fundraising, and sharing information with newspapers, or otherwise reporting to the news media. In our plan for direct-democracy, by contrast, limiting each person to one proposal at a time means that that one proposal will receive much more attention from its author than a congressional representative or senator could ever devote to work on legislation. In a direct-democracy, those who propose changes to medical malpractice, for example, are grouped together with other proposal sponsors who also proposed changes to medical malpractice. Unlike the Medical Committee in Congress, these sponsors will only discuss and study their one chosen field or aspect of medical services, and this means that they become medical legislation experts. The same will be true for people making proposals for health insurance, laws about the uninsured, and other medical legislation. Through this plan for direct-democracy, the number of proposals each subject may receive remains virtually unlimited, and the reason for this is that whereas each person is limited strictly to one subject, the number of people in the nation that may pursue changes to existing national laws is also virtually unlimited. Our solution utilizes well what most people today regard as a weakness and turns it into a strength. For example, our illusionary thinking could be that we have a world with so many unique, totally different people, with so many unique, totally different concerns that it must not be possible for all these different, unique individuals ever to work together well.[58] If you can access the unlimited potential of a single person, can you fathom the unlimited potential of all the people? The solution is to turn the necessity in a democracy for more hands in the law-creation process from a perceived weakness into a strength. After all, God commanded each person to meditate on the law day and night.[59] Ultimately, this new method is designed to have better-educated ideas through a higher-level of specialization among those ideas. It is important to remember that genius does not come from knowing everything well, but rather from understanding something from one aspect of a subject that others have missed or overlooked. Consider Henry Ford, he was the genius behind the mass production of the automobile, but knew very little about the planets or biology, whereas John Washington Carver was an expert on the soybean but knew next to nothing about automobile assembly. The genius of these people and others like them was that they could take a single subject and research and study it well enough to see something that others missed. It has been said that Einstein got so caught up in the experiments he was working on he forgot how to tie his shoes. The more people we have invested in the process, the greater availability and specialization of the ideas that become available to the public.

In the Republic, on the other hand, on the Medical Committee, one member may have his primary desired focus on malpractice, another on HMO reform, and another on options for Medicare. While it is true that their medical knowledge and interest may, in each case, be specialized into some medical field, when it comes to actual cases, each of their specialized interests may be in different areas than in those that they came formally to consider. Thus, while they may be well-suited to discuss and otherwise deal with Medicare reform legislation, they wind up making key discussions for multitudes about medical malpractice, about which their knowledge may be scant, or the result of politically motivated hearsay. Because there is only one Medical Committee, such legislators are left to study whatever is the topic at hand. It may be true that Congress could form a second committee on Medicine, but this could produce friction between the two new groups, and political considerations could thereafter dominate the discussions—and the decisions. In a direct-democracy, on the other hand, there would be, for example, medical malpractice proposals grouped together by libertarians who proposed them, a different set of malpractice proposals done by liberals, conservatives, or lesser-known political groups, such as osteopathic physicians. Direct-democracy takes our accentuated human abilities with the advantages of specialization to a whole new level. The key difference is that now the public has the right to choose which path the nation will take, and it does this through the endorsement of particular proposals. This way, even in a world with billions of people, laws are still created that directly reflect the wants and wishes of the all, and of the cast-aside person.

The movement from Republic towards Direct-Democracy began many years ago. These theories we now discuss are only taking advances we might term evolutionary

[58] Pure democracy is collectivist mob rule, <capitalism.org/faq/democracy.htm>.

[59] Deuteronomy 6:4-9; Joshua 1:8; Psalms 1:2, 119:97.

advances, moving ahead by their own internal logic, incrementally, progressively to their next, higher level of development. Direct-democracy does not have the built-in disadvantages we have mentioned but instead takes the dedicated special interests directly into account, turning them into virtues, which moves the whole legislative process ahead idealistically, to a higher-level for the good of all. Yet we know that there may be thousands of people in these industries and services across the country that want deeply to change those enterprises and industries in which they now work. What remains important is to make an accurate determination about which proposals are best, and to distinguish them from those of little merit. Therefore, like shire proposals, those who make national proposals must also meet with the *causa enim novo* trial in their own shire and there argue their case before a jury of peers. Only those people who can obtain approval for their national proposal by securing a majority jury vote may then move onward through the process, advancing their proposal. Like local proposals, national proposals too must go before a review board before they go to trial. This process of review, discussion, and debate through the review board and the trial ensures that the proposal does have merit and that it has the potential for community approval even before it comes to compete with other proposals on the same subject. Collectively, with separate proposals all on the same subject, each potentially vastly different from one another, bring together for a collaborative discussion with all the groups of concerned citizens that are most passionate and focused on the work at hand. This is analogous in the republic to the subject focus and the legislative purposes of the various congressional and parliamentary committees. To some degree, like the members of Congress, these people got their original authentication from the people. However, unlike those members, their original approval came not from a vote for office by their constituents but directly from the subject matter of the proposals upon which they themselves have worked to advance. The genius of the people is therefore brought to bear directly upon legislation, rather than blunted obliquely, masked or diluted, as is much more likely to happen in the republic. Direct-Democracy is not therefore aristocratic in some of its impulses, but rather it directly trusts the people—all the people.

Mergers and Modifications

In a direct-democracy or a republic, bringing all the people together to vote is a major challenge (if not an ordeal), and therefore typically it is done—in the United States at least—only twice during election years. Therefore, it is imperative that the measures placed before the public be both comprehensive and well considered. To vote on every one of these proposals is not practical, although each proposal represents some person's creative thought and unique viewpoint on the issue in question. Considered individually, each proposal may seem much like others or be distinctly unique, and it represents some perceived need seen as understood by someone. When these ideas are then considered together and comparatively, a more comprehensive and complete view of their subject emerges than from whatever emerges from the usual deliberations done in a republic by their legislatures or congress. Individual proposals seldom discuss the many possible alternatives, and the solutions they offer are but rarely comprehensive. We must also consider the obvious fact that the number of national proposals that can go onto any ballot is limited.

A democracy carries with it another challenge that a republic does not have. Because a republic limits its power to the one philosophical element with a majority of members in congress the legislation presented is always within the framework of that political sphere and does not face competition from other philosophical rivals. However, in a democracy it is possible for multiple groups to submit vastly different pieces of legislation on the same subject within the same ballot. This creates a real problem, because under such circumstances as the people have passed both propositions and both are now the law, which takes precedence? To ensure this does not take place the national ballot is limited to proposals that do not conflict with one another on the same ballot. Beyond that, let's say healthcare Proposition A becomes law during the primary election in May and is set to take effect the following year. Yet, before proposition A takes effect competing healthcare Proposition B is placed on the ballot in November and passes during the general election. Such a circumstance would throw out Proposition A even though it passed through public vote and had never yet been tried. Thus, I have put forward the following further stipulation, that between directly competing proposals on the same subject only the one with the most signatures will be placed on the ballot and will be given a full election cycle to prove its worth before being faced with a proposition to reform or eliminate it. I realize that extraordinary circumstances are available due to the unforeseen consequences of new laws, but barring such immediate risks each law has a right to prove itself. Also, the signatures of the competitors are not lost. Those proposals may continue to evolve and change in the background until their time comes.

This means that the effort put into the signature-gathering process, to get a national proposal onto the ballot, would have to be major, or extensive. Because of the numerous requirements, these proposals must meet to get onto the ballot, and become propositions; all of them must compete with others, as the proposers struggle for that final official status for their measures. By allowing national proposals to merge, therefore, the result will be tangible, practical benefits. When two national proposals become one, then there is the potential for the signatures gained from each to be joined together to underwrite a new single, more comprehensive, unified proposal.

While modifications are important, mergers have several superior attributes when compared to modifications. While it is possible to modify the proposal with the strengths of another through a modification, to do so loses an ultimately greater strength in the value of the mind or minds that originally conceived the proposal from which the modification is drawing new knowledge and learning. When a merger is performed, the entmoot of sponsors and cosponsors from the two previously separate proposals, now have the benefit of new minds who may see the proposal in a different light. Of course, differences of opinions are difficult to overcome, but our new entmoot is still in general, aiming for the same goals and objectives as the subject matter of the proposal remains constant. Each potential problem brought to light by these new members, while it involves struggle should be viewed as a potential opportunity to improve upon the proposal. In this way a competitor is transformed into a collaboration for the ballot. We also realize that as the number of sponsors grows it will become exponentially more difficult to modify the proposal, due to acceptances of mergers and modifications requires four-fifths of the sponsors and cosponsors to move forward with any merger. This allows each entmoot to develop a natural equilibrium, in terms of the number of sponsors they feel comfortable with. By design, this allows the proposal to gravitate toward greater amounts of stability as the proposal reaches maturity. With the passage of time, this should naturally create a demand in society for larger and larger collections of sponsors and cosponsors per proposal, as competition increases to reach the ballot box.

Among the arguments to a Republic is the sheer quantity of laws that come out of congress each session. However, while there are significantly fewer propositions on the ballot in a democracy, each one of those propositions has been theoretically refined by their sponsors and cosponsors for years, perhaps decades. This process will make each proposition significantly more thought out and comprehensive of the industry. Consider healthcare. A proposal may start with healthcare, but as one digs into healthcare they may find issues with health insurance, which may lead to questions about life insurance. Out of health care may lead to questions about mental health and out of that may envelop psychiatry. Perhaps drug addiction or prescription drugs. One may ask questions about the healthcare for the homeless or immigrants coming into the country. Perhaps epidemics, medical privacy, international medical collaboration, and research. Perhaps veterinary medicine, from their natural preserves, and wildlife protection. Thus, while there are fewer bills, those that make it to the national ballot are infinitely more comprehensive and intricate. Research on any subject is seemingly endless, because just when you think you have everything, something you never thought of comes along or perhaps technology changes in some way that alters your course. This is what it is like for one person researching a subject, but imagine a bill with a thousand signers, perhaps a million. Because they are invested through their endorsement each signer is going to have their own opinions and insight into every aspect and alteration. While the public knows little about what is really going on in their legislature, in a democracy as bills grow sponsors and cosponsors can expect a deluge of emails and correspondence from endorsers and potential endorsers all rendering their opinions and insights on the proposal. Considering the division of the public into realms of study the knowledge base of each citizen will also be infinitely greater. My prayer and hope is that in time mergers will cross the philosophical divide as groups begin to see the wisdom in their rivals. Thus, the quality of each piece of a legislation in the end will be beyond anything the republic could ever hope to achieve. Considering large portions of society with a direct-representation government will now be involved in the law-creation process we can expect with the passage of time society will gradually become more tolerant of their fellow man, because intolerance will limit those in society from competition in the law-creation process.

Therefore, just as I urged humanity to travel the square, slowly the law creation process will also travel the square until topic by topic, issue by issue, the number of proposals will begin to diminish. Once democracy is unleashed and a world that has been denied a voice suddenly achieves one, political solutions like new Industries will erupt with a flood of competitors. Like anything new and novel it will attract a large portion of the population. But as its awe and mystery dissipates and the true work that is involved in the process is realized the men will be separated from the boys.

During my life, I spent many years in technical support. It became apparent that sales had complete control over all product research and development. I noticed that support would frequently complain about some flaw in the software. I made the case to management that sales could get new customers, but it was the task of support to retain the existing customers. If the customers are turned-off by a specific issue, we may lose repeat business. I recommended that tech support be allowed to vote on the greatest issues in the product each month. And the one or two with the greatest majority would be sent to programming for repair. Management agreed. The first month I got good participation. The second month only three of the ten support representatives participated in the vote. By the third month, through the sixth month, I was the only voting member. From that point on anytime I heard a complaint I would offer the employee the option to submit their proposal, but once the reality of the work involved through programming and testing became apparent participation dropped. On the positive side, though staff was not participating they liked the fact that the option was there. Complaints subsided. And employees had a more positive view of the organization. Also, one by one the initial issues presented were addressed over the course of the next year and sales growth followed.

Thus, the process not only weeds out bad proposals, but through time enhances the quality of both sponsors, cosponsors, and signers as the reality of the process is understood. And even among those who choose not to participate, the mere fact that they could means something. In our polarized world it means something that the public can do more than just complain.

There is another irony. Generally, I found the more communication between departments and management the less communication was needed as trust pervasive and good faith was felt by all. On the other hand, the more restricted communication between departments the more the perceived incompetence in management and the more disenfranchisement among the employees. Primarily when people feel that they are a slave to machine, rather than a fundamental organ of the organism. For instance, in support I discovered the installation manual was incorrect on several points. Though I was not allowed to cross departments to talk to the tech-writers I did anyway. They conveyed to me that they were also restricted from talking to engineering and so had to make several assumptions about how the product worked. I secretly intervened and re-wrote several installation manuals. Management didn't find out about it till the customers began to call back with high praise. It is because the public does not trust their elected officials that they take to the streets to demand change. If the laws passed through the people are a positive, fewer people will participate in the process. However, when things go awry participation will naturally increase to the degree of public satisfaction with the system. Though the process may be long, as is the nature of capitalism, there *will* be winners as the public's demands are met one by one. Yet laws will have flaws and will need to be updated from time to time with new legislation. Until a monopoly is created, however, in the law creation process the victory is not economic but victory over the mind on any specific subject. When the end-result satisfies all holistically a Liberation of Consciousness occurs, and transcendence follows to the next plain of human existence. Jezreel is not the destination, but merely the path to the oneness of humanity. The oneness of humanity is the elusive pot of gold at the other end of the rainbow.

To achieve the rainbow all of humanity must feel connected. How the sponsors and cosponsors treat those who disagree will be viewed by all. Thus, a word of advice for the sponsors and cosponsors, no signer is worse than no signer. People will forget what you said, people will forget what you did, but people will never forget how you made them feel. The worst of all outcomes is when the public goes silent, not because they think everything is going great, but rather because they are disillusioned with the system as a whole and believe they are helpless to make a positive change. Or even worse the public feels they will be repercussions for themselves or loved ones if they take a stand against some form of perceived injustice. The people who signed these original proposals are not just silent partners in the merging. Those who chose to sign the proposal must be allowed to view the proposed modifications and then be given the opportunity to resubmit their signatures. Modern technology makes it possible to send out thousands of emails in a matter of seconds to alert all those who might be interested in the proposed changes. Still, *we, the people*, must have the choice either to receive or decline these emails so that these messages will be received rather than automatically rejected and left unopened as spam or junk mail. To enable these processes, the Willow Wisp realm is responsible to create a website, or latest technology of the modern age, where *we, the people,* may log in on our own time and at our personal convenience to see the proposals that would require, for a merger or modification, the resubmission of a signature, etc. Every signature is important, and this process ties the whole legislation creation process directly to the people. We accept the fact that many signers may freely submit their signatures without a proper review of the proposed legislation. As always, this must be their own choice, but there will be many others—the politically responsible—who will participate in the entire process with a sufficient *gravitas*. Because there are these more serious and socially responsible people, it is expected that the sponsors and cosponsors of any proposal will seek feedback from those who endorsed their proposal with their signatures prior to any mergers or modifications. In the republic, there are many pieces of legislation that pass through their legislatures virtually unnoticed, some for the betterment of society, and some not. The merger process is vital to allow each proposal to be as comprehensive and as complete as possible so that ultimately many minds that have the same passion about the subject will further refine it, to make the best bill possible for the people. In theory, this procedure will provide all qualified voters with a voice in the law-creation process (which is always best), and those who submit proposals are directly dependent on the people for their individual proposal endorsements and prior suggestions to achieve, finally, best-possible legislative propositions and laws.

When we contrast this process to the law-creation process of the republic, we find conversely that in a republic the people themselves are involved only in the hiring process of their elected representatives rather than with the actual creation of new legislative proposals. This is not to say that the public cannot write their representatives if they dislike legislation, or if they have ideas they see as better, but rather the representative has been elected already when national proposals for laws are being written by Congress. Obviously, members of Congress are not directly dependent on the will of the people when they compose, write, or pass legislation. Recently Congress attempted to pass legislation requiring that persons or organizations who ask others to contact their elected representatives must register as lobbyists. Sadly, nowadays, some members of Congress put letters from their constituents into the same mental compartment as spam or junk mail; they consider it a nuisance. Such tendencies reflect the ever-widening gulf separating the few with power and influence in affairs of state and the ever-increasing masses of powerless have-nots.

If Jezreel is to survive and succeed, it must be built on the involvement and direct participation of the people in every way, but most especially in the law-creation process. Through the legislative modification and merger process, we seek to maximize this involvement and the people's direct participation. Of course, there will be issues and disadvantages with this solution. For example, some sponsors will issue modifications or accept mergers too often, others, who may be too eager to please, will accept any change blindly without proper research, and still, others may become unreasonably and rigidly resistant to any subsequent proposal modification to their baby. Having considered all these possible variations on a theme, we must still ponder the basic instincts of our species. People who become too rigidly possessive about their proposals may never get enough signatures to compete in the process, and those who accept change too readily by way of being too eager to please everyone will lose the attention of their endorsers. By allowing people to be themselves, the natural processes will work best. We are reminded here of what Sigmund Freud's great colleague Alfred Adler said in his advice about raising children, *"Make your child independent!"* and also what Montaigne said in general, *"Let's allow Nature to have her way, for she understands her own business far better than we do."*

This process of merging similar proposals ultimately will reduce the number of national proposals, thus providing more comprehensive solutions to the public while also retaining better the representation of the people who themselves sponsored those proposals. With the number of national proposals across the whole country, those who chose to sponsor a proposal have many other national proposals from which to choose when they are considering a merger of proposals, together with the required signatures.

The Marathon

Admittedly, this task is overwhelming for sponsors and cosponsors who are essentially working pro-bono. Just as it was with local proposals, the more national proposals there are on the ballot, on the average the less attention each one will get from the public. Due to the reach and scope of national proposals, a limitation per election year. This limitation should also take into consideration the amount of change that each proposal brings to the table. The more change, the greater instability that proposal could potentially bring to society. Therefore, the greater the change-rating the Causa Enim Novo jury gives the proposals, the fewer propositions are on the ballot so that each proposal gets more scrutiny and attention. Of course, when it comes to local proposals, the people themselves have the final say through the vote as to how many propositions may be placed on the ballot.

To accomplish these basic goals, we need to do several things: First, we need to increase the inherent worth or value of the national proposals as submitted. By limiting the number of proposals each person may submit to one, along with having tangible consequences for abandoning proposals, the proposal process is opened to everyone while also serving to focus each person's attention sharply upon some chosen subject. With the website I am proposing feedback methods and channels for the free exchange of ideas and debate. What we hope to accomplish thereby is to make the law-creation something like going to college. You can do it, but before you enroll, you must think long and hard because then you are committed.

After a person has submitted a national proposal, we must assume that he or she is one of many throughout the country who has also submitted such national proposals. These people individually have little chance of seeing their own national proposal eventually reach the ballot box. Therefore, there should be some forum for those proposal submitting people to see what other subject-related national proposals are out there. This will be needed if we are ever to have any hope that well-integrated, related proposals will merge.

The Internet, by its very nature, is virtually open for all. Of the technologies available, it is the only one that would allow national proposals to be viewed collectively by society. We realize, too, that there could be, possibly, thousands or even tens of thousands of proposals out there awaiting consideration. Therefore, the first need of any such online service would be to categorize the many individually submitted national proposals. To be user-friendly, the online forum would have to allow search options with search engines like those of Google or Yahoo that achieve a ranked priority, which in this case would be determined by the number of signatures already achieved. Such simplicity would allow anyone, with just the click of the mouse, to read any national proposal submitted, or any number of such nationally submitted proposals. This would enable a proposal submitter to gauge and compare his or her own ideas with those of other similar national proposals. If, after looking over another national proposal online, that person agreed with the logic of that other proposal, he or she could communicate with that other proposal sponsor to discuss or negotiate a possible merger. So then, with this process, the more mergers a national proposal would get, the greater the momentum and visibility that proposal would have before the public. Consider, for example, the merging of five similar, like-minded national proposals. Four of the five proposals may have sponsors or cosponsors who could not even imagine ever obtaining enough signatures to get their proposals onto the ballot, but if one of the national proposal sponsors does eventually succeed, then all the national proposals that previously merged with that one have, in a sense, some potential to ride onto the national ballot box. This is important for several reasons. People often come up with amazing ideas, but then later, after some discouragement with their implementation, they relent, settle for less, forget, or finally view their original ideas as fleeting pipe dreams. But with this better and more carefully established plan, if an idea does have real merit, our procedure carries within itself the greater potential of having someone else notice its merit, and then possibly want to merge that proposal with his or her own. This blending-and-merger process is much greater than that, for as the merger obtains unto itself not only the better ideas so appropriated, it also fosters the creatively shared decision-making process itself, as people learn better to share their ideas, hopes, and dreams with other proposal submitters and sponsors. Creative teamwork and collaborative networking abilities are fostered. Having achieved a shared goal or vision of a better future, the entmoot learns how to work together better. To encourage this process merging proposals do not have to go back to the Willow Wisp Courts for review until a proposal gets close to obtaining the number of signatures to reach the ballot. And then the trial is only done for a review of the change ranking and potential competing proposals of the same rank and subject. My hope is that this process of revealing to the sponsors who their direct competitors are may foster bipartisanship through mergers, rather than further competition where only one of the proposals would be permitted on the ballot during any specific election cycle.

Learning to work together for the common good is wonderful, but at the same time, it remains important that people should not become blind to potential challenges likely to arise in the proposal merging process. Dissenting voices that are heard or unheard may make the final difference between a good proposal and a bad one. To amplify the voices of dissent, we propose a four-fifths majority vote among the cosponsors to accomplish any proposal merger. Secondly, if a person removes cosponsorship without clearly stated reasons, then the person must wait three years before sponsoring or cosponsoring any other proposal. However, if the person submits the proposal to public dissent and debate, he or she may cosponsor or sponsor a proposal after only one year. These provisions do several things: First, when it comes time for the trial of other mergers or of the merger itself, it gives the prosecution (which is against the proposal) a great deal of Insider Information about the proposal itself. It also gives the prosecution a witness who can testify against a proposal or a proposal merger. Therefore, it is beneficial for all proposal sponsors and cosponsors to listen carefully to any complaints among their own internal discussions. At the same time, this careful listening (and with appropriate responses) prevents the dissenter from removing his signature of approval from the proposal for merely frivolous reasons.

It is also important that national proposals be well-rounded. That is, they need to reflect the needs of the entire nation, rather than those of only some select region. This is one of the strengths of the republic as a government system, because, for example, the U.S. House of Representatives has elected representatives people from every part of the nation. This accomplishes several important things: It binds the nation together (underneath or behind the legislation passed), and it also tends to make legislation less provincial because congresspersons from other locations may voice their complaints and constructive criticisms about any proposed legislation. In a direct-democracy, it is equally important that the people from the nation have a voice in the national proposals that are submitted. Therefore, I propose the following rule: When a national proposal merges with another national proposal, it shall receive an additional ten signatures per jury member who supported the proposal, provided that the merger represents proposals from different shires, or if an additional twenty-five signatures per jury member (who originally supported the proposal when the merger occurred) represent proposals from different states. In theoretical terms, what we thereby attempt to accomplish is to make it more immediately advantageous for proposal sponsors and cosponsors to look carefully into the ideas and the national proposals submitted by others from across the nation. These procedures should also help to reduce local prejudices and promote a broader and more informed cosmopolitan, mutual understanding between the diverse minorities we tend to find in many modern societies.

Every race has its starting line and its finish line. In our race, the starting line is when the courts come with their verdicts that the proposals pass the Causa Enim Novo, and the finish line is when the proposals become propositions on the ballots. Even after the union of as many as five proposals, there could still be hundreds or even thousands of proposals circulating. However, because there are only a limited number of proposals that may be placed on the ballot, this makes the race for the ballot box a long and arduous competition. But there is something here that is profound: While it is true that there may be stiff competition among the many various proposals, society will over the course of time begin to build a unified consensus around the proposals they most favor. This process in and of itself will move society away from competition between and among people as candidates for political office, as in the republic, to a much healthier competition centered on, and revolving around, ideas for legislation that move the society ahead. With this major advantage, also, we have the basic fact that the more signatures a proposal gets, the more public recognition and debate that proposal will have received, and rightfully so.

Our focus nearing the final stages is on the competitors among national proposals to become propositions on the ballot. Working together as a team is still to their sponsors' advantage, and the more unions their proposals make with other proposals, the more signatures they will each have; and this, in turn, will give them a tactical advantage by moving their proposals ahead of some of their competitors' proposals. This process will also reduce the total number of proposals, which, in today's age of information overload, will be much better for the average voter.

Yet there are several other components that need to be analyzed. Laws are still best done at a local level. Therefore, we need to have some safeguards to protect the rights of local governments. The closest representative or symbol of local law is the town mayor, however, because this is a kingdom, I will refer to the town mayor as the town lord (though this lord has no nobility, but is an elected official). Regarding the lord and the shepherd (our regional governor), while we would like to believe that most political officeholders would want best results for the people, we must be realistic and believe that all politicians—good or bad—being politicians, naturally will want to secure and build their own power. It is important that these natural instincts be utilized in the service of the public. The more power that goes to the national government, the less power the lords will have, and therefore the fewer powers, rights, and privileges the people of that city will have. For this reason, the lord should, if desired, be allowed to hold town-hall meetings on any proposal originating from the public signature-gathering process. To ensure that the lord does not abuse this process, the lord may perform only town-hall meetings on proposals that already have passed the Causa Enim Novo trial. This procedure ensures that proposals will originate from the people rather than the lord, and it also provides a method outside of the Internet that the people in any city may use to learn more about proposals circulating among the public. If the people attending the town-hall meeting favor the proposal, they will sign it, but if they do not, they will not. At the end of the meeting, the lord will be given an opportunity to cast his vote for the proposal publicly. If the lord signs the proposal publicly, a thousand signatures will be added to it. This is done for several reasons: First, it gives the lord a significant incentive to open the lawmaking process to the public, with free debate, which goes beyond the online forum. Second, it is highly unlikely that the lord would advocate or endorse proposals that diminish the local rights of either himself or the community's citizens. This measure provides the lords with an incentive to get actively involved in law-creation. Such involvement is encouraged naturally from town-hall meetings, which empower the people to make informed and intelligent decisions. Like our senators under the US constitution, the lords function in the law-creation process to retain the powers of the local government to the greatest possible extent. However, the lord, unlike a senator in Congress, is available to his community because the lord lives and does business locally instead of far away, in the nation's capital. Best of all, unlike the situation of senators, lords gain power as their cities' powers increase.

There is another important note between a republic and a democracy. In a Republic the Representatives are voting for or against each proposal, but in a Democracy the citizens are only endorsing the proposals they like, they are not actually voting against them. Thus, there is a positive tone throughout the process. Yet there needs to be an option for the public, not necessarily to vote no, but to publicly provide a reason behind why they are withholding their signature. Afterall if a citizen thoroughly researches the bill and through that process discovers a major flaw the public has a right to know why they did not sign. Thus, the public can give a rank of each proposal on the Willow Wisp website. Similar to how products are ranked on Amazon. Five stars for awesome proposals down to one star for flawed proposals with the option to leave a comment. The public is free to sort comments by star ranking to see the proposal underneath the hood so to speak. Of course, the sponsors have the right to address each concern through explanation or modification. The public in turn has the right to be notified of their response and change or re-post their rank and/or comment.

In theory, what we attempt is a completely positive evolution of the U.S. Constitution. Under the US Constitution, the two law-creating bodies were the House of Representatives, to represent the people at large, and the Senate, to represent the rights of states. Therefore, the natural evolution of the House of Representatives is towards more and better representation by simply allowing the common person to represent himself or herself. As for the Senate, the natural evolution is towards the shepherd (governor) or the lord. Between these two, the lord is the preferable alternative because the lord is naturally much closer to the needs of his or her own people. Unfortunately, as the population expands continually, even the lord's ability to see and understand what is going on locally becomes impaired to some degree with the increase in sheer numbers. Although for now, the lord remains the best alternative.

The chances are that a lord usually will not call a town-hall meeting for a proposal unless the lord feels that the proposal has at least some hope of success. Therefore, the initial start in the race will always begin with the will of the people, as was the original idea behind the House of Representatives. Again, in these matters the larger historical trend we follow, we would argue, is simply the natural evolutionary trend of the United States Constitution, which is by now long overdue for its next major advance.

As the proposals accumulate signatures and reach that final stage toward the ballot, it is expected that they will receive multiple levels of merger requests from related proposals as their advocates attempt to get them past the starting line. We need to remember that these sponsors and cosponsors are not paid members of the government. They are voluntarily putting forward a proposal they believe is in the best interests of the nation. Most, as it is expected, will still have to earn a living by some non-political means. Many will be family members with the responsibilities of child-rearing. The process of reviewing these merger requests can be overwhelming and detrimental to the proposal itself. After a proposal has attached so many signatures, qualifying for a degree or *powers of authority* proposal, the prospect of losing those signatures, so that the signatures must be resubmitted due to a merger, places barriers against the proposal itself. In some respects, this is healthy because it allows the public to gain understanding without viewing the proposal as a *moving target* due to its constant mergers and alterations. Having said that, I do not want a merger request to be off-handily rejected. As proposals near the finish line, probably they will be featured in the news media in the same way that legislation does as it makes its way through Congress. Unfortunately, as often occurs with members of Congress, after going to a few media interviews, many become arrogantly imbued with the idea that their own ideas or opinions are better and more important than the ideas and concerns of others. To keep the sponsors and cosponsors appropriately modest, as well as to ensure that they analyze each prospective merger that is sent to the sponsor and cosponsors, there must be consequences not only for accepting a merger proposal but also for rejecting one.

To accomplish this suitable modesty, with any merger of a proposal that is rejected in the next *causa enim novo,* the prosecution may subpoena the sponsors or cosponsors who rejected the merger to have them testify against it. This allows the prosecutor to bring in a field expert to testify against a proposal, but it also provides, at least in theory, that the sponsors or cosponsors will not reject a proposal without solid grounds. It is expected that multiple mergers may be attempted and rejected. This allows the prosecutor to subpoena different witnesses from several different aspects of the proposal on trial. Such trials are expected to have media attention. For sponsors who rejected a merger on solid, reasonable logic, while the trial will not be on the sponsor's proposal, it will be on a similar related subject. If the sponsor's logic against the proposal is viewed, as having merit, it will further create creditability among the public for his or her own proposal, possibly increasing signatures and visibility among the public. On the other hand, sponsors who reject a proposal without knowing all the facts or as dictated by logic, or according to what does not seem reasonable to the public will tend to diminish the credibility among the public for their own proposal through their own short-sided actions. There are also other considerations. If a sponsor from *Proposal A* rejects a merger with *Proposal B* to preserve the signatures that *Proposal A* has achieved already, the sponsors of that proposal may lose signatures because the sponsors and signers of *Proposal B* merger rejection may have signed *A* as well, and now, just to protest, may withdraw their signatures.

There are still other matters about this process that we must consider. The four-fifths majority vote required for a merger or modification was intended to make it difficult for the shepherd to have an intimidating dominance over the proposal itself. Each merger adds to the total number of sponsors and cosponsors of a proposal, which also makes each voice in the proposal proportionally smaller, and the voices of dissent larger, and this process is itself like what happens when the number of legislators in a congress or parliament increases. If a proposal with a limited number of signatures say a hundred, merged with a proposal close to a ballot initiative, say 500,000 signatures or more, then the original signers that have fought through the signature-collection process are given an equal voice to those that have just joined the process. Due to this, It is expected that many proposed valid mergers will be lost because the original sponsors and cosponsors of the proposal do not want to lose their voice over the proposal itself. To help work around this dilemma, we create the ability to do mergers based on *nonbinding sponsorship.* Nonbinding sponsorship allows the proposal to merge but does not allow the sponsors and cosponsors of the proposal with fewer signatures to have a voting voice in future mergers or modifications. Nonbinding sponsors and cosponsors may, of course, opt-out of the merger and remove their sponsorship if they find the terms of any future merger unacceptable. It is still important for the proposal's original sponsors to listen to their nonbinding sponsor's contributors because they are also tied to the life of the proposal itself. Should any Nonbinding sponsor or cosponsor opt-out of the proposal, they may still be subpoenaed to testify against the proposal concerning future mergers. Such testimonies by their nature will spike passions of a dramatic nature that the press will love, but they may tend to lessen public support for the proposal in question.

Perhaps Nonbinding sponsorship seems cold, but when one considers that proposals near the finish line may receive hundreds of merger requests and are putting forward their proposal through voluntarily means, this prospect and endeavor will not be easy. A legislator in the U.S. Congress, by contrast, has virtually no consequences for ignoring a citizen or multiple citizens in his or her district, and they are paid for what they do. The distinct difference is that the people involved will be every day, concerned citizens. Inevitably, many of these people will become famous, not by financial gain or through the powers of office, but by their ideas and the struggle that surrounds those ideas for precedence. What is the definition of a hero? Consider soldiers, nurses, and scientists. Heroes are people in society who are instrumental in achieving ideas, often at great cost, that are far greater than they are.

This new method of government has been designed to bring these everyday heroes to the attention of our children to emulate as role models. Every public trial as the proposal moves toward the ballot will bring with it media attention that will also tend to amplify public discussion, but unlike the present government, if a person agrees with the idea, he or she can take positive steps to support the proposal just by adding a signature. However, this leads us to another real danger. This gives the press a great deal of power to amplify the proposals they agree with and to suppress the proposals with which they disagree, simply by not airing them. The press gets ratings by printing what is popular, or whatever will draw an audience. Consider a nation at war where that nation is in the wrong, and a foreign power was right to attack: Would the press cover that story? Members of the press are people just like everyone else, and sometimes they allow their own bias or preconceptions adversely to influence a story. The press also acts as a corporation, not an impartial third-party, which means that those running the corporation may filter the information they receive and then reorganize and publish in ways that suit their own interests by making it more colorful or controversial rather than telling it plainly, and without such hyperbolic distortions. *Time Magazine* used to run an advertisement boasting, "*Time* makes everything more interesting—including you!" Yes, I would agree. They did and still do make many things "more interesting." At the same time, however, there is such a thing as *responsible journalism*, most journalists usually try to adhere, at least mostly, to that professional standard, and the free press has always been one of the cornerstones of any free society. The basic, underlying challenge is that the free press usually does not envision its professional role as providing leadership for the communities it serves or for the kingdom.

National Public Decrees

There are several insights about humanity that through history, have proven themselves right over and over again. As a species, we long for, and strive to, enhance our own individual existence, both for ourselves and for our posterity. This natural struggle is essential in any democracy, it is healthy, and it has allowed our species to adapt successfully on this planet throughout the ages. Unfortunately, that same natural drive sometimes has impelled political leaders to overstep their boundaries, shortcut their ethical obligations, and impose their personal wills over society wrongfully. Having said that, we also know that for any society to function, it must have effective leadership. There must be someone to man the oars on the ship in distress, to fly the warplanes in times of war, to bring aid quickly when natural disasters strike, and other such speedy defenses and rescues that are expected of all governments in times of disaster—what we refer to today as leadership. The question then turns to how to maximize the voice of the people to the shepherd through a venue outside of the law creation system. China in its meteoric rise on the world stage created a social media platform between the people and the government as a means of voicing public complaints about the existing system.[60] The government is required to publicly respond to each complaint. Through similar systems each realm may be driven by the public and allow the public to feel that they have a voice in the

[60] Liuyan.people.com

system. It also provides the shepherd a gauge of what needs attention and the urgency of the attention required. The shepherd as an administrator thus can administrate his realm to the best of his ability with a focus on management rather than law creation.

There are still lessons to be learned from our earliest ancestors. When the designers of the Constitution created the role of president, the president's position was never intended to be a part of the law-creation process. Congress was intended to be separated as the law-creating body from the President because the law was intended to be a check on the powers of the President to keep him or her in line. Ergo, having the President submit legislation to Congress, was akin to asking the fox to guard the henhouse. The only reason the president was given the right to veto legislation was that the designers did not want the president to be forced to enforce laws he believed were unconstitutional.[61] Therefore, the president could veto any legislation crossing his desk that he believed violated the Constitution. This concept only lasted until the Andrew Jackson administration. President Jackson started the inevitable process of vetoing legislation just because he did not like the legislation. Like most powers taken by those in authority, once taken power is rarely given back without a struggle. Presidents began to use their powers, along with their veto power, more obviously for purely political purposes, to reward and gain favor with their constituents. Unfortunately, we know that our instinctive drive as human-beings for whatever is better may take the form of wanting to increase our own personal power illegitimately, for the wrong reasons. It is also true that in times of crisis, a nation looks to its president for leadership and solutions. On a Biblical level, these same powers were also separated. To Levi, the Levitical Judicial promise to enforce the law through the courts, to Judah, the Davidic powers of leadership, and to Joseph the Jezreel powers of the people. And has prophetically occurred God has Divinely granted Joseph, our people's component, powers over Judah and Levi.

In the Republic of Switzerland, the people have the final say through the power of the vote about whether a proposal shall become law. However, they are voting on initiatives put forward by their congress and not the people. The only true solution is to have a wall of separation between the national leadership and the people as the law-creating body. To accomplish this nine months before an election the national proposal with the greatest ratifying signatures from the public will be slated for the ballot without intervention from the national leadership thus creating a government for, by, and of the people. As this takes place and the media begins to stir over the coming election six months prior to the election another proposal, again, the one with the most ratifying signatures, will be slated for the ballot.

This also brings us to another fundamental problem that also exists in the republic. The laws are intended to originate with Congress, but due to the increasing powers of the president with the passage of time the gradually diminishing role of individual

---

[61] Executive Branch, president designed to enforce law, not create it; <bensguide.gpo.gov/9-12/government/national/executive.html>. Rethinking the presidential veto, <law.harvard.edu/students/orgs/jol/vol42_1/broughton.pdf>. The increasing powers of the president, *The American Dream*,<chaosacrossamerica.com/AmericanDream.html>.

members of Congress, the president's ability to present legislation to Congress, and when his party is in office see that proposal become law. Such powers and central control reflect a government that is incrementally devolving its way back to its primitive monarchical origins. In a direct-democracy, there is no Congress, for Congress is the people. For this reason, each national position of power, which we refer to as Shepherds. Each Shepherd has a separation of powers from the other Shepherds of the land, each with a specific area of jurisdiction held in place through the competition of the Shepherds and if that were not enough, each Shepherd has an opponent, a Guardian to ensure the Shepherd does not violate the rights of the local government and the private sector which I will discuss in the next section. To ensure this, national public decrees are limited to two types. First, national decrees related to the halo under the jurisdiction of a specific Shepherd or shepherds as well as restraints on their power. Second, Collective Responsibility detailing responsibilities left to the shire and local government as well as how the shires and local government function between themselves as well as between it and the other halos.

There are other threats to the people as well if the shepherd could introduce a proposal and then publicly gather signatures using the national media spotlight, available to most high-ranking elected officials, to the shepherd's proposal, we risk undermining the authority of the people to create law. Remember, in a republic, the president was not formally designed in the constitution to initiate legislation, but today, contrary to the intentions of the designers of the constitution the president, rather than Congress, has become an integral part of the presidential candidates' campaigns, when they run for office. If the media attention available to the president is so bright on the president that it often leaves members of Congress in the twilight or shade, struggling for attention, what would this mean in a democracy where our law creators are ordinary citizens, next to the prestige of the shepherd's office? The shepherds, like the president of the republic, have been designed with the domestic responsibilities of the president to enforce the law rather than create it.[62] To allow the shepherds to present legislation from the top-down, instead of originating with the people from the bottom-up has the potential to turn the shepherds into monarchs, just as has become the case with the president in a republic. This problem runs deep because it is instinctively natural for people to want to expand their own authority whenever and wherever possible. To prevent this from happening, the shepherd may not sponsor or cosponsor any proposal after assuming office. The public may determine what the penalty for such crimes should be through powers of authority proposals and by the Guardian, which are matters we will discuss in the next chapter, and as pertaining to who will be responsible for enforcing such laws.

In compliance with the principle of the two levels of Congress, each national proposal must also receive support from at least three-sevenths of all the shires in the nation. This will ensure that national proposals receive support from the majority

---

[62] Executive Branch, president designed to enforce law, not create it <bensguide.gpo.gov/9-12/government/national/executive.html>. Rethinking the presidential veto, <law.harvard.edu/students/orgs/jol/vol42_1/broughton.pdf>. The increasing powers of the president, *The American Dream*,<chaosacrossamerica.com/AmericanDream.html>.

of its citizens, and from both metropolitan and rural areas of the nation. Notice that it is possible for a Kingdom Decree proposal to pass without a majority of shires if it can obtain a majority of the popular vote.

Our north star in these matters is that all law is better, the closer it is to (of, by, and for) the people. For this reason, too, we allow the local law with the most ratifying signatures to be placed on the national ballot. Astute readers, you will recall that a proposal, if it passes in one shire, may be put on the ballot in another. This way of copying proposals over the course of many years may get the law passed locally in five, ten, twenty, or even more shires. A nation, however, may be made up of hundreds, or even thousands of shires. Fundamentally, we know that all law is evolving. We do not want laws created on a local level to cause divisions between the shire governments. We are faced, therefore, with an impasse. How can most of the law-creation process be kept local to retain good participation and representation of the common person, while still providing unity and coherence among the various shire governments? By allowing one shire law as a proposal to all shires, the law remains local because each shire may choose to accept or reject the law. This procedure allows the most popular shire proposals and propositions to be seen across the nation. For shires that pass propositions, in those shires they become law. For shires that do not pass the proposition, the law will be revoked, thus uniting and maintaining continuity at the local level through a uniform set of laws.

Is Unity at Odds with Representation?

We have established that governing more horizontally, from a shire level, grants more representation than governing from far above (a state or national level). This will inevitably bring us to another major dilemma facing all attempts to achieve a direct-democracy governing system, which is that while local governments gain more freedoms and are therefore better able to represent their populations, local governments while becoming more distinct and unique in the way they resolve the issues they face. This uniqueness, while it may enhance creativity and good representation, also naturally increases the dividing lines between different shire governments, as they become increasingly more distinctly different. Laws made at the state-level rather than the shire level may be less representative for the average citizen in the state, but state laws unite the shires under one set of common laws, which facilitates mutual understanding and cooperation. The same may be said about laws created on a national level for this reason: The national government removes the representation from the individual states, but it also unites the states under a set of common laws. As we survey international relations today, one main reason we have wars between different nations is that their separate national laws allow them to develop differently, and there is little or no adherence to international law where they do exist, or enforcement of those laws, to tie and bind them more together or encourage similar, parallel development. This amounts to an inverse relationship. Jefferson saw the relationship between local government and national government this way: *"While smaller governments are better adapted to the ordinary objects of society, larger confederations more effectually secure independence and the preservation of republican government."*[63]

National laws create a cohesive, united country working within its own national boundaries, but as such provide far less direct-representation than laws created by cities and shires. Should more enforceable international laws ever exist, it would serve to bind the nations together, but if done incorrectly, the effects upon representation could be catastrophic. One of the basic theoretical challenges with international law or world government is that if the international authority figures become corrupt, or the system otherwise breaks down, there are no other countries to which people might flee to escape oppression. Shire laws, while they do provide the most direct and best representation with diversity, also lack the unified coherence that state and national laws provide.

The designers of the American Constitution also faced this dilemma. Like republics of the past, they used the lawmaking power of Congress to create national laws that would bind the nation together. Yet the designers of the U.S. Constitution knew that those with this power, through the Congress, to increase their own power, could work long-term to erode the rights of the people, as they had experienced in their own history with the English Parliament, where they were not represented. Parliament had passed the Stamp Act and other colonial tax laws that provoked the original Americans who responded with the American Revolution.[64] For these reasons, the Constitution designers set into place several barriers that would serve to hamper such developments. Some of these barriers included certain rights reserved to the states, individual civil liberties, the president through the veto, the Supreme Court as a distinctly separate governmental branch, as well as other checks and balances, as well as other agencies and institutions, the political functions of which we shall examine.

In any event, the law-creation process itself, whether it is for national or local law, must begin and end with the people rather than with a set of elected officials if we, the people, are going to achieve a true Jezreel. However, right away, we face the puzzle of which laws should be national and which local. The law-creation process itself is limited by how many proposals one may place on the ballot. If the focus is moved to national law, then once again the majority of the nation's people will have no real voice in the law-creation process. In addition, in this process, the rights of the minority shires disagreeing with the national initiatives will have their representation diminished. Of course, it is important that the kingdom endures as a united whole, but it is equally important that the national government become not so powerful that it can circumvent the law-creation process itself, as it exists for the cast-aside person.

Historically, when we analyze what the original form of the United States government was, we can see similar ties set into place between the national government and the state governments. These original ties from the United States Constitution were developed to bind the nation together, while at the same time restraining the powers of national law that would separate the cast-aside man, in

---

[63] In Defense of Democracy, <etext.virginia.edu/jefferson/quotations/>, Letter to William Stevens Smith (November 13, 1787), quoted in Padover's *Jefferson on Democracy*, <en.wikiquote.org/wiki/Thomas_Jefferson>.

[64] The Stamp Tax, <usahistory.info/American-Revolution/Stamp-Act.html>.

terms of the law-creation process, from active participation in law-creation. Essentially, all the other rights were left up to the states or were given to the people, stated in the Tenth Amendment: *The powers not delegated to the United States by the Constitution, nor prohibited by it to the States, are reserved to the States respectively, or to the people.*

The *Jezreel Constitution* establishes limitations on the rights and abilities of the national government, and how that government may interact with foreign nations, as well as the protocols and priorities in relationships between the city and shire governments, and the protocols and priorities in relationships between the shire governments and the realm governments, which is our evolution of the state government. To better comprehend this evolution, consider that in historical times people communicated through proximity, in that mountains and rivers prevented daily dialog between people living in different geographical areas. Thus, with time the laws within these areas evolved differently so that for instance the law in early New York was very different from the law in early Georgia. In modern times with the arrival of the internet this has migrated from geographical boundaries as a historical state divided to mental boundaries or the way our own passions divide us. In that we are dealing in the realm of the passions of the heart and imagination. In our new modern paradigm often, a person will know and can describe in detail their thoughts within their own niche, be it religious, political, professional, etc., and ironically not know the name, political thoughts, or outlook of their next store neighbor. Thus, we are labelling realms domestic geopolitical needs that go beyond the scope of the shire government. Such realms may include higher education, power generation, agriculture, etc. Like a state there are natural boundaries within the sphere of influence of each realm. Yet we are migrating away from the physical boundaries of the state to the geopolitical boundaries of the given realm limited only by its budget and need within society. Anything not listed in this document as specifically being a right for the realm or national government is to remain the right of the shire government, whereby the bulk of all law shall be left up to the people through self-determination by means of their shire vote. In the words of Jefferson, *"Congress has not unlimited powers to provide for the general welfare, but only those specifically enumerated."*

With the long view of history, we have seen and understood that merely stating that the Constitution limits the national government to the powers it specifically enumerates is not a sufficient safeguard because inevitably the national government will always attempt to expand beyond its preordained and, as it may seem to us, *natural* boundaries. Most of the rights in contention stem from those granted to Congress in the original Constitution, under Article 1 Section 8: *The Congress shall have the Power to lay and collect Taxes, Duties, Imposts, and Excises, to pay the Debts and provide for the common Defense and <u>general Welfare</u> of the United States; but all Duties, Imposts, and Excises shall be uniform throughout the United States.*

This one phrase was the core around the anti-federalist argument against the Constitution, and why the Bill of Rights was constructed, especially the Tenth Amendment in favor of the rights of states. James Madison, the author of the Bill of Rights, expressed the worry of the anti-federalists this way: *If Congress can do whatever in their discretion can be done by money, and will promote the General Welfare, the Government is no longer a limited one, possessing enumerated powers, but an indefinite one, subject to particular exceptions.*

Unfortunately, for constitutional scholars, the term *general welfare* is rather vague. To help alleviate this ambiguity, we need to understand the context and concerns of the original Constitutional designers. Through the study of history, we find two distinctly different arguments about the need to put this phrase into the Constitution. The first argument was that there was a need at the national level to provide for projects that would bind the states together, such as a national road system, a postal service, and later projects such as the telegraph, the telephone, and others. The second argument in favor of the general welfare clause had to deal with the size of some of the states and their relative inability to deal with natural disasters or medical epidemics. For example, if a major earthquake were to hit Los Angeles or San Francisco, California is a large enough entity in terms of both size and population to be able to deal effectively with such a crisis without having to turn to the national government for help. However, when Hurricane Katrina went through New Orleans, it overwhelmed the levees, leaving enormous devastation far beyond Louisiana's ability, financially and in other ways, to cope. This meant that assistance from the federal government was immediately vital to millions of lives. The possibilities of disasters like these, whether or not they are directly man's doing, left the designers with a dilemma: The larger a state is, the more self-sufficiently it can provide resources for use within its own infrastructure, whereas a state with fewer people can provide better representation for its people. Rather than force the smaller states to incorporate with the larger ones, they allowed for the national government to step in during times of crisis, and they worked to connect the states together through roads and communication technologies. They also had another dilemma in that they did not know which technologies or kinds of crisis would come after them; hence, the wording *general welfare,* deliberately leaving the term ambiguous for the future indeterminate needs.

In this new system of government, we face the same dilemmas as did the designers of the original U.S. Constitution. It, therefore, becomes important for us to amplify the positive, cohesive benefits of the larger states while at the same time not losing the better and more direct-representation provided by the smaller, less populous states. To accomplish these ends, each realm embodies the whole of the kingdom, but each is limited by its jurisdiction. For instance, our Atlantis realm is responsible for the nation's water supply. Everything from flood control channels, dams, aqueducts, dredging, aquafers, irrigation, etc. Because there are no state lines to its jurisdiction states are not completing over water resources but rather shared for the betterment of all. Other realms reflect the kingdom's power grid, communication, and transportation. Thus, our goal is to divide the national governments power into independent realms of cohesive uniting jurisdiction held within their jurisdiction through the competition between realms. Rather than a singular national government, independent realms will have the infrastructure and resources in terms of major highways, ports, colleges, aqueducts, irrigation, and other needs that are beyond what is practical for independent states to handle today. See the dynamic at play, the law-creation process for the most part exists on a shire level, with smaller populations and geographical size, such as Rhode Island, Delaware, and Vermont, which are vastly smaller than our new form of realm government, allowing the representative needs of the population to remain close to the people, within their local communities. In this manner, we can amplify the benefits of both contrasting needs through our new form of larger realm government, thus removing the needless ambiguity of the *general welfare* clause, by removing many of the emergency infrastructure and medical response needs from the present national government to the independent realm governments.

The original design of the United States kept in mind, allowing for competition between the states, whereby people would be drawn to those that they believed provided the highest quality of life. The major preoccupation among the anti-federalists was that the term *general welfare* would lead inevitably to the creation of a national government monopoly of power, thus eroding and then voiding healthy competition between the states, and now, in the present age, once again we have this major concern. James Madison, referring to the general welfare clause, said, *with respect to the words general welfare, I have always regarded them as qualified by the detail of powers connected with them. To take them in a literal and unlimited sense would be a metamorphosis of the Constitution into a character which there is a host of proofs was not contemplated by its creators.*

Collective Responsibility Laws

This view of the Constitution, however, leads to a problem for which the anti-federalists were not prepared. If we were to take the Constitution as it was originally designed, needed national programs such as Social Security, Medicare, and Medicaid, would all be unconstitutional. The problem with monetary competition (an effort to keep taxes and spending low to attract business and industry, etc.) among the various states rather than a competition for the betterment of humanity (ending disease, poverty, suffering, etc.) was that if a state did provide these needs for its people (such as with Social Security or Medicare), many people needing various kinds of help the state provided would flood the state, all of which could make the cost burden upon one state exorbitant. By moving these needs to a national level, the kingdom can take on the financial responsibility for these needs without any one state having to assume the whole burden. The argument today between constitutional scholars is not that these needs are not there, but rather that the national government should not have a monopoly power to provide for those needs.

To better understand this dilemma let's consider a debate within the modern era. One can read all the books on becoming a parent, but nothing can truly prepare one for the experience. It is an exhausting task with an extensive learning curve. With the cost of housing increasing as well as years of college required to get into a good career people are becoming parents later in life and thus no longer have the energy they had in their teens and twenties to keep up with an average toddler. To alleviate these needs parents often provide self-entertainment activities to toddlers through television, video games, etc. As the methods for self-entertaining have increased exponentially childhood friendships from the neighborhood have correspondingly decreased. Beyond this, the number of children in an average family has been steadily decreasing over time so even sibling interaction has decreased significantly. What becomes neglected is the interaction with other children which plays a huge role in the development of language and basic social skills. This along with environmental and technological factors which are pure speculation at this point has made autism the epidemic of the modern age. One of the solutions to combat this epidemic is to provide pre-kindergarten childcare programs so that children have extended interaction with other children along with other activities to stimulate the social aspects of the mind and assist with early diagnosis. Because new parents are unaware of what normal should look like most diagnoses currently take place at five years of age. This is because when a child enters Kindergarten the comparison between students becomes dramatically apparent and the school district takes notice. However, by then the core developmental years of language from ages three to five have been lost. Some of these children never fully recover and the system is faced with a lifelong burden.

On the left, the solution put forward is to provide federal funding for preschool and early childcare. Because K-12th grade education is a right of the local government the right sees it as a breach of their state's rights in that their local voice in a democratic fashion is excluded from the process. Due to that exclusion, there is a fear that parents will be forced into the process of raising their children in a manner through a federally mandated system that may be out of sync with the parent and local society's belief systems. However, if any one state or local community provides for these needs they risk an influx of those with the needs migrating to their community without the financial support to meet that influx thus creating a push for a federal solution which in turn violates the local rights of the state and local communities to have a voice in how their tax dollars are used as well as a voice in the education of their children. Beyond that if the state and the federal government are considering providing the same services the state becomes more reluctant to invest for fear of a duplication of effort that may put all the state's efforts in the proverbial wastebasket should the federal government step in to meet the need.

So then, once again, we face a real dilemma. How can we provide for the obvious needs of the elderly, the poor, and the disabled without violating Jefferson's direct-democracy goals, in terms of the representative rights of the local communities in their shire and city governments? The solution, I would argue, is to create national laws that represent a collective responsibility to the individual shire governments. Thus, from our example above if approved by the people all shires would share an obligation to provide Pre-K education, but how that mandate is enforced and carried out would be per the local laws enacted by the people within that community. Collective responsibility laws have been divided into three forms of responsibilities: (1) the local government budgets, such as the city budget, (2) the collective responsibilities of business, and (3) collective individual responsibilities. To understand better how these three forms work, we may illustrate their differences by applying each form to the medical community. It is possible to provide health care through the city budget, thereby ensuring that all members of the community receive medical attention when necessary. Of course, if there is a natural tragedy, such as with severe weather, the state government also has a responsibility to assist. Second, health insurance could be provided through the business community, as is the present system with federal employees in the United States today. Third, the kingdom could move to an individual health savings account plan, which would make each citizen responsible for his or her own health care needs. Finally, the kingdom could use a combination of the options above. Since health concerns are universal, or, at least similar everywhere, whichever direction a country takes, the people themselves through their own national vote should determine their own degree of coverage and which of these forms of responsibility are most prudent for their own society.

The first option of, leaving the responsibilities between the local governments, equal to their population and standard of living is equally good, and many cases may be the superior option because the people in those shires may decide for themselves how to meet these needs through a shire vote. However, there are issues with this option, as well. Consider Social Security and Medicare as possible examples of programs which may be better served through the local government, rather than through the national government. Most people in New York live there because of the employment options in the state. However, the cost of living there is also higher than in other states, and many people who spend their entire working life in New York eventually retire in Florida or other states with a lower cost of living. This dilemma was not anticipated by the original Constitution designers because in the day of horse and carriage travel was comparatively difficult and time-consuming. What once took days or months may now be done in hours, such as in one evening, without missing work time. To make Florida responsible for all the retirees coming in from New York State would remove a great deal of the responsibilities from New York to its people, and at the same time force huge responsibilities upon the state of Florida, thereby exceeding its means. The solution, in this case, may be to hold the local government responsible for providing savings to be used toward retirement for the years' people worked or lived in the jurisdiction of that city or shire. Therefore, if the people of that shire voted to weaken such laws, they would only be hurting themselves.

This, however, leads us straight into another dilemma. Some have stated that providing social security from the individual places a person has lived and worked throughout his or her life is becoming more impractical and bureaucratic, as we move toward a society of greater ease of movement and transportation, however such arguments fail to consider our technology through computers and online documentation has also advanced allowing us to track and streamline such activities with ease and efficiency. To further work around this dilemma, we stipulate that a person has the right to receive his or her funding, whether it is Social Security or Medicare, from the shire government or city government in which the person lives, and it shall be the responsibility of the city government to collect the funds from other cities or shires in which such people have lived. This is preferable, rather than have the individual bear this responsibility, for in this manner if the hosting city or shire cannot collect it, they eat the loss, not our elderly poor person barely subsisting on regular social security payments. It is also important to remember that if a city or shire attempts to renege on their collective obligations, that these laws are established through national law and should the city or shire attempt to circumvent the system the city or shire will be going against the shepherd whose jurisdictional responsibilities is to ensure the law is enforced. Now, whether Medicare and Social Security should be handled in this fashion is not a constitutional question, but rather a question to be determined by the people. I only point this out to show the while local power and authority is paramount for achieving the closest will of the people if the holistic needs of all shires are not considered, the results could be disastrous.

Now, for this to work properly, national collective responsibility laws must allow for some flexibility, to be determined by the people of that shire or through the city budget. At the same time, the collective responsibility laws must be strong enough that the shire governments do not neglect their financial obligations to their citizens or make such collections too bureaucratic. To that end, if a lord believes that a national proposal, prior to passage, is inflexible, then the lord may call a town-hall meeting where he or she, after hearing the concerns of the city's people, may veto the proposal. However, a single lord may not veto the proposal without publicly doing so by going before the people of his or her city to explain his or her logic, as well as allow his or her constituents to respond before the veto is issued. Only then does the veto become effective for that lord. In addition to that, a full 40 percent of all lords in the country must convene town-hall meetings and then veto the proposal for the proposal itself to be fully vetoed. The lords are also obligated to do this before the proposal becomes law, for in this way the proposal may be modified and thus address the lords' concerns before being placed on the ballot. A lord's veto will remain on all proposals vetoed, regardless of modifications to the proposal, until the lord rescinds his or her veto or until a newly-elected lord for that jurisdiction publicly rescinds the original veto through another Town-hall meeting. Going back to the original American Constitution, we remember that although the president was granted authority to veto legislation that he sees as unconstitutional, the states (through the Senate) still had the power to override the president's authority if the senators believed that the law was in their state's best interest or to preserve states' rights in general. This way, the federal government allowed for the powers of the states to have supremacy over federal powers if the states' rights were on the line. We are attempting to put the same principle into effect here, such that if a national law carried enough potential to undermine local representation or to place financial restrictions on the local government greater than its capability, the lords would have an opportunity, before their people, to put the brakes on those national proposals until the needed changes were made. In the end, it is the people who will decide whether the national legislation placed on the ballot is the right course of action. Sixty percent of the lords throughout the kingdom is a large enough proportion, meaning that only in extreme cases would the lords be collectively able to use this authority. Then, if even 5 or 10 percent of the lords put forward a veto, although it would not be enough to stop the legislation from going to a public vote, still it would create national headlines. This would also allow for the concerns of local governments to be heard and perhaps heard enough to provoke changes to the legislation proposed or to change public opinion, which might be just enough to vote down the disputed national proposal.

Having said that we must consider that there is a fourth option and that is to place the responsibility on the government of the realm. For example, it is possible to provide healthcare through the realm budget as determined through a Kingdom Decree. This Kingdom Decree is not within his or her realm only but rather is voted on by the entire nation for national law. This is because while local governments are designed with a great amount of autonomy to preserve their individuality, while the realm governments I designed to unite the kingdom together. Yet we want the realm to also maintain a sense of individuality and uniqueness. Each realm has been given a specific area of responsibility, but that specific area of responsibility is kingdom-wide. Therefore, we use the term realm and not state as realm implies a completely different dimension or area of study, so that one of the realms may be tasked with meeting the healthcare needs of the kingdom, while another that of aqueducts and water treatment, and still another prisons and rehabilitation. This specialization allows each realm to remain unique and focused on perfecting one aspect of the kingdom, and because that specialization is Kingdom-wide each realm in its own way serves to unite the kingdom. This fourth option is not without risks as it removes the ability and voice in the local governments to modify or alter the law as may seem fit to their culture or customs. It also carries the risk of growing the power of the government of the realm and therefore, the Shepherds of the Roundtable. To limit these risks, we have placed one stipulation that collective responsibility laws that increase the responsibilities of the government of the realm through the realm budget must be free to the public in that no form of charge or tax may be levied to use the service provided. This means that to provide for another responsibility in the government of the realm budget, the existing responsibilities must be altered or shrunk. This ensures on some level that existing programs under the realm budget will be continuous and constantly under scrutiny by the public hoping to add new programs in. A primary example of the use of such a law would be the national highway system, which is the responsibility of a specific realm for the entire kingdom. While a person must pay for the vehicle they drive and the gas they use, a person does not have to pay for using the roads each time they get on the freeway. Consider telecommunications, the responsibility of yet another realm, in the same light. Telecommunications companies receive funds from the government to put up telephone and internet lines that they charge the public to use. This is to say that the taxpayers are paying his or her telephone company to use the same lines they paid to install. It may be easier to allow the government of the realm to upkeep and expand the phone network so that the public only needs to pay for a telephone and then all the calls inside the country (or even perhaps through agreements with other countries) would be free to the people making and receiving the calls. Like the freeway concept, such system would serve to increase business and commerce throughout the nation.

Cable and Satellite TV (or Radio) are other industries that could also be considered for such integration into the realm budget. Paying for movie channels that have no ads is understandable, but why should the public have to pay for TV with commercials? Understand I am not referring to the kingdom paying for government Television, which under all cases should be through the private sector under the laws governing the freedom of the press, I am only referring to the method by which the channels are received. Should the public have to pay the cable network to receive channels, when that cable network was installed and paid for through their tax dollars? Also, consider that like the highway system, the initial cost is high for construction, but maintenance of the existing system is very inexpensive. The existing cable companies collect revenue from the public for usage of the cable lines long after they have been paid for.

Consider the internet industry. The government can install a large antenna that provides internet coverage to the public for multiple miles at five-percent of the cost than the alternative that is in place now where each family pays for the coverage of their own home. Which method would best serve the needs of the public?

Because the national budget increases with unemployment the shepherds can have a highway, the Internet, Cable TV and other infrastructure projects put together in advance so that as employment needs arise through the country's infrastructure projects can immediately meet some of these needs in an automated fashion. Default unique and individual kingdom-wide responsibilities assigned to each realm are found in the next section dedicated to the capitalist in the chapter on Fantasia, such that one realm is responsible for the healthcare needs of the kingdom, while another is assigned transportation infrastructure, and still another communication, etc. However, these options are not set in stone, rather they are alterable so that if the public decides to privatize for-profit or through not-for-profit one realms responsibility they are free to do so, or to assign it a different fundamental responsibility, or to re-arrange or reassign the individual responsibilities as the people see fit for their welfare and for that of the kingdom. Some of these other options available to the public, related to healthcare, for instance, I have just mentioned. This is not to say that this fourth cumulative option is the best option and should always be used, but only to show the positive options that may come from such an option and why we have allowed such an option in place at the realm level and why it would be detrimental to personal liberty to deny this option to the people.

Ultimately, and what is most important, is that any Constitution must layout the specific rights granted to the people, along with means to enforce those rights, to ensure that the sovereignty of the people themselves is well maintained. These rights are so essential that we specifically mention them because we do not trust the national government to allow these rights to be preserved simply by virtue of their not being mentioned specifically in the Constitution. These are the same elements spoken of in the Tenth Amendment, namely, the rights of the shire, the evolution of state government from its original Constitution, and the separate rights of the people.

When we analyze these elements in the US Constitution, we can see that it is defined and defended clearly by way of the original composition of the United States Congress. The division of Congress into two different parts had many purposes, but among them, the most fundamental purpose was that the designers believed that this separation and distinction would best preserve the representation and rights of the common person. These two elements have been considered by many to be the lost two elements of the lawmaking process: the states and the people. By design the House of Representatives was elected by the people to preserve the rights of the people, and the senators were elected by the state legislatures to preserve the rights of the states, as expressed in Article 1, Clause 3, of the Constitution: *The Senate of the*

United States shall be composed of two Senators from each State, chosen by the Legislature thereof, for six Years; and each Senator shall have one Vote.

While the designers understood that many elected representatives do not go to Congress specifically to preserve their individual rights of the *cast-aside* citizen, but rather they go to express and act upon their own ideas, dreams, and goals, and they also believed that representatives elected to the House acting outside of or beyond the will of the people would be removed from office through the vote and that senators who did not defend the sovereignty of their state would similarly be removed from the Senate by their state's legislature. To see these matters clearly, it is helpful to know that the people who were running for office in those days were putting their own lives and the lives of their families at risk: During the Revolutionary War, for instance, several early legislators had their homes burned or all their earthly possessions stolen. These first legislators were not affiliated with any political party, and their seat in the Continental Congress was often without pay. Those were difficult times, but later studies show that these very perils much enhanced their quality of service by, in effect, adding courage, integrity, and determination to their job requirements. Consider the speech made by the drafters of the declaration of independence urging the delegates to sign the document. As the day wore on the issue hung in the balance, and then, according to the story, a man rose in the small gallery. He was not a young man and was obviously calling on all the energy he could muster. Citing the grievances that had brought them to this moment, he declared:

> *Sign that parchment. They may turn every tree into a gallows, every home into a grave and yet the words of that parchment can never die. For the mechanic in his workshop, they will be words of hope, to the slave in the mines—freedom. If my hands were freezing in death, I would sign that parchment with my last ounce of strength. Sign, sign if the next moment the noose is around your neck, sign even if the hall is ringing with the sound of headman's axe, for that parchment will be the textbook of freedom, the bible of the rights of humanity forever.*

Then it is said he fell back exhausted. While there were political parties outside of the United States, such as England's Parliament, made up of Whigs and Tories, in America, the foundational structures of the political party systems were not developed until after the ratification of the Constitution in 1787 and 1788. The Constitution, for example, has no structure for primary elections wherein the political parties select their candidates prior to the general elections. However, where such gaps existed the natural evolution of the republic as a form of government filled that void.

Party Politics

As a part of this study, in 2018 I ran for the US Congress to get a first-hand experience of what it is like for political candidates and how the process works or doesn't work. How does the public get a real understanding of the candidates in order to select the ones that will be committed to writing the best laws? First, I discovered a large percentage of lobbyists who if I agreed to be their puppet, would give me their endorsement. When I read through the voter pamphlet to see where my opponents stood, I discovered that the incumbents and party faithful would submit a volley of endorsements from various groups in their write-up, so I really had no idea of where they stood, but only who had bought them off. Of course, the biggest doners such as AIPAC are not displayed. While the common working-class person just trying to make a difference would courageously open their heart to the public in the voter guide. Granted the guide only allowed for 325 words, which I guess is better than nothing. Yet through an online voter guide a person's passions, without the word limitations of a paper guide, could be put on display for all to see. This however is not what the parties want, because to do so may reveal breaks in the ranks of management. In an effort for full disclosure in the guide I referenced a previous version of this book. From my write up on the next page one can see I used every one of those 325 words. To make this more evident various organizations would give you a questionnaire to gather your opinion on various issues, but they would not be looking for real answers, but rather Yes or No answers to leading questions where commentary was not allowed. When asked what was most important to me, I stated the freedom of Palestine, to which they responded that option is not in the list. You must choose something else, such as: abortion, gun control, etc. which are distraction topics meant to redirect public discussion away from topics the binary system doesn't want the public to discuss, such as the genocide they are committing in Gaza. Thus, rather than serious issues candidates will look for topics that provide zero contention with the party faithful. For instance, the incumbent's primary topic was opioid addiction. This too was an effort to mask how she got elected and where her loyalties lie. In the previous years when the Portland City Council passed BDS legislation she was one of the minority city council members who supported Israel. AIPAC picked up on this and she got a free ticket into congress where she used the national government to undo the decision of the Portland City Council. Realizing that she obtained her position essentially through a bribe she sticks to party line talking points and questions on the middle east are avoided like the plague. Yet, her voting record tells a very different story. Today when I am given a question it takes me time to weigh my response against my years of experience, thus I may need to take a step back and contemplate before I give an answer. Such is not afforded a politician. Rather the politics of a republic have descended into a world of stereotypes. People's entire career is summed up in one label, ultra-liberal, extreme right-wing, etc. Such oversimplifications of a person's humanity denies their individuality and only serves to build collective animosity. To change the rules of the game I called out the establishment on the one subject that I was an expert at more than any other. So the debate would not descend into anarchy, but rather be based on the merit of each argument I selected the Lincoln Douglas style of debate. This style is preferred because it allows each side uninterrupted time and each purely responds to the statements of the other so that they may get deeper and deeper into the issue. Also, the time allotted was much more than a thirty-minute debate but three hours in length. Furthermore, my challenge was to the best of the industry, against one person myself so that they would have the benefit of collaboration. I paid for everything. Yet with all the advantage of the theological foundation of thousands of years as well as all their combined experience they did not have the courage to even take the stand.

US Representative, 1st District

Michael Stansfield

Democrat

Occupation: Author

Occupational Background: Dreamer(Birth-Present)

Educational Background: Self-Taught

Prior Governmental Experience: Citizen

In the West Bank, I visited Al-Fara Detention Center where Palestinian children were tortured; I went to villages where water and pastures were poisoned to expand settlements, among other atrocities. The UN, established by the US, has documented multiple violations. Once verified, Europe responded through boycotts, divestiture, and sanctions until violations cease & resolutions are enforced. Netanyahu used anti-boycott laws to silence opposition. Through the Anti-BDS Acts, cosponsored by Wyden(S.720/S.170), Schrader(H.R.1697), & Bonamici(H.R.2856) AIPAC lobbyists seek to establish the same censorship here. H.R.1697 hinders the UN's Human Rights Council's ability to investigate and act on abuses for one nation alone through personal fines of $250,000-$1,000,000 & 20-years in prison. H.R.2856 overturns the rights of business & industry.

Civil Disobedience: I declare my support for the UN, EU, & BDS, as part of the Methodists UN affiliation, demanding that all commerce that contributes to human rights violations be made public. Any censorship of atrocities becomes a license to torture & murder with impunity. Everyone must have the right to advocate against any product for any reason as well as to know if an organization has committed human rights atrocities. Our representatives are signing over our rights to allow a foreign power to suppress knowledge of their crimes and prevent any response. No foreign power deserves such a right against humanity.

Why are things this way? In our Theocracy, one race is deemed chosen, while another is damned, granting preference to Jew over Arab. Evangelicals will not allow any Biblical discussion that favors the Palestinians. Among these are Gregg Ramona, Athey Creek, Multnomah, even George Fox. These experts are just part of the underlying intolerance that is on the verge of legally suppressing our speech. Before passage, I am calling them out for a Biblical debate over Zionism. Free admission, May 1st, 7PM-10PM, Sherwood Arts-Center.

You are my jury. Vote your conscience.

(This information furnished by Michael Stansfield.)

Real knowledge and wisdom take time. Bring out the details of any subject and see the true wisdom of the individual. It is much easier to see all the things a person is against, but this negates a better solution, which is why one is electing a congressional candidate in the first place. Thus, how can I create a better and more efficient law writing and creation process to ensure that the details are not missed but amplified as part of the process.

The political party system, by dividing and segmenting political philosophies each into their perspective areas, gives the cast-aside person a general idea of where the candidate stands on the issues. The media has already conditioned the public within their respective philosophies so that those that run for congress neatly fit into one side or the other. Thus, by association and broad-brush labeling the members of each party feel a passionate alignment with their elected officials of whom they don't truly know. Of course, the reality of the human heart is not so neat along party lines, yet to maintain their position in the party the individual divinely created variances of the heart are suppressed. To do otherwise would undo the public myth. Ironically the candidates who are true to themselves are painted as those who betray the party's core beliefs. For instance, all the Republicans who voted to impeach Trump for the January 6th insurrection would lose their seat in the primary election. Rather than challenging the myth and accepting the reality that the true enemy is their own suppression of the heart all wrath is redirected to their philosophical rival. Anytime you divide groups by philosophy and then dangle power and authority between the two groups you are going to create an atmosphere of animosity and contention. During the early history of the United States, the staff of the entire federal government was let go everytime power changed hands because one side always believed the other side could not be trusted. By like standards during the Iraq War President Bush of the USA let go of the entire Iraqi infrastructure, because they were members of Saddam's Baath (Renaissance) political party. Among the many drawbacks from this is that all the experienced members of each branch of government are lost. It is as if the system is starting from scratch with all the problems that learning something new entails and, of course, like all changes these things just swing the pendulum from one form of persecution to another form of persecution from another administration looking for payback, justifying wrongs committed under the guise that the other side is much worse. One of the obvious examples of this was in South Africa after the fall of Apartheid mass numbers of people were fired from positions at power plants and government institutions because they were white, shifting from one form of discrimination over to another. The US solution was to take politics out of the situation so that only the department heads may be changed out during a transfer of power.

Nowadays, candidates often attribute their political success or failure to the party system itself, rather than to the voters, because the parties provide most of the funds that get them elected. In addition, political philosophies, within the larger framework of the political party systems, seek continually to amplify their own power, which tends to amplify the power of the party system itself. Those in Congress in opposition to their party on individual votes may see their funding diminish. The Squad, for instance, was a group of Democrats in Congress that stood against the genocide in

Gaza. The president oversees his own political party, and his primary contributor was AIPAC, therefore because the president can regulate the amount of funding that goes to individual candidates in his own party, and as he is not going to go against his donors', members of his own party get caught in the crosshairs. Because Congress sends billions in foreign aid to Israel each year and those funds come right back into their campaign coffers from AIPAC lobbyists the entire apparatus becomes under the control of a foreign power, because to deny funding to the foreign power or admit to the bribery scheme is to out the party system and all who are a threat to the party get crushed.

The idea of democracy is powerful. There is a reason the primary government model in the world is the republic. As a carrot on a stick the US has dangled its model of government to poorer nations saying follow us and the prosperity of the United States will be yours. Yet in secret the US is laughing and mocking them. Through manifest destiny, the United States, in its pride, has set itself up as superior to all other nations, in both ideas and wealth and only seeks to use these nations for its own ends. Even as one could consider them the childlike offspring of America. America, like all nations, does not like to consider that other nations have come of age and are acting as a counterbalance to its own power and control over our world. Yet the Kingdom of Heaven is forcibly advancing. With Gaza on the proverbial cross the manipulation of the United States is on full display. The people within the United States can see it is blatantly apparent that their representatives have been bribed by Israel and do not represent them. The Global South can see how the entire world is manipulated through the US veto power in the United Nations and how the CIA has been manipulating nations through coups to get leftists out of power in poorer nations allowing the US to feed its capitalist engine. Yet in doing so it has built factories and industry around the world to the point where the US has become the obsolete business partner. A sponge that in relaxation and comfort takes all the profit without meaningful contribution. Now that the veil is lifted the full scope of the tyrant is revealed as it tries to maintain control it has rightfully lost. It is as if the world has been unionized against her.

The movement to free Palestine and end colonialism as demonstrated through people taking to the streets around the world is democracy in action in its truest form as the people try to take back their rightful place. In a true democracy, there is no congress, because the people are the congress. The law creation process has been given over to the people and there is no reward for party affiliation. Unlike a congressional representative, there is no need to suppress the truth because your proposal belongs to you and is a representation of you and is thus independent from any political party affiliation. If there is a congress of sorts it is within our evolution of the Senate through a collection of lords aka city mayors throughout the kingdom and their vote, unlike a Senator in a far-off capital each vote takes place before a townhall meeting so that the city lords are directly accountable to their electorate. Their power is also limited, as the law creation progress starts with the people and the final vote is also through the people. In the early history of the United States, as time passed, people could see that a select few heads of the political party system were maneuvering the members of the Senate like puppets on strings; it was the old tale of Adam Smith's invisible hand at work. Therefore, an amendment to the Constitution was advanced to alter the election process of senators, who previously had been elected by their state legislatures. Now, they were to be directly elected by the people through the vote. At the same time, by moving the election of the Senate to the direct vote of the people, the tangible link between the states and the federal government was removed.[65] Most, unfortunately, this left the states with no way to directly enforce their rights in the national government.[66] Thus our goal is not to create a law creation process among the city lords, but rather a method to ensure that the rights of local governments were not infringed upon, but encouraged.

To begin to understand how to unravel and solve these challenges, we must look at the ways nations have already developed to combat this loss of representation among the people and their rightful place in the law-creation process. One method, as previously mentioned, was the development of the state propositions. By this means, with enough signatures, a cast-aside person (i.e., someone without special political powers or influence) could get a proposal onto the ballot for a statewide vote, but even this comparatively straightforward process has several complications. People can put on the ballot only proposals over which the state has rights. As the national government increases its powers, fewer and fewer powers are left and available to the people at large, because the state itself has fewer rights and powers. The challenge for the people gradually becomes worse, too, because increasingly and inevitably we find that organizations, especially wealthy persons, and the most powerful corporations pay for the collection of signatures. Then, the widespread use of this process gradually has increased the number of signatures normally required to get a proposition onto the ballot. As time passed, it became more and more difficult, if not impossible, for the cast-aside person to put his or her ideas or daily concerns onto the ballot for a vote. If we look at these developments, it becomes apparent that the signature-gathering process must remain local for the people to have any real voice regarding which proposals are selected for the ballot, as well as input into the process of creating law, if the ability to change society in meaningful ways is to remain accessible to our *ordinary person*. Historically, we see that removing the link between the states and the national government through the direct election of senators left the national government, rather than the states, in charge of uniting the nation, which meant increasingly remote representation for the many, but also a more unified federal government and nation. However, when the unity of the nation is not through the people it is not a democracy, regardless of the claim by those in power. The result is always tyranny at the top through an abuse of power usurped from the people. As an individual's power diminishes, their ability to live up to their potential erodes slowing society's pace of efficiency, science, and technology. Those at the top, regardless of the prestige of the office are given an ever-greater burden of power beyond which honest men and women can live up to. Thus, the positions of those in congress and senate transition from the law creation process to purely a process of obtaining power through endless campaigning and competition with political rivals

[65] Repeal the 17th Amendment—<articlev.com/repeal17.htm>.

[66] 17th Amendment, Federalism— <//liberty-ca.org/seventeenth_amendment.htm>.

with many speeches about law creation, but little change beyond the status quo and when change does come it is mediocre at best.

The original intention of the American Patriarchs may have been that the states could choose to be a democracy united through a republic that was merely a collection of states. As the national government assumed more power in and of itself and the power converged within the two-party system the state rather than look to the people for their power all eyes were fixated on the top of the chain, because that is where the true power resided. This was not always the case. Prior to the civil war all eyes were on the state governments because they were the real source of power. Functionally considered, if we were still living under the original United States Constitution, in which people voted into office their state legislature, which in turn elected its two senators, the state legislatures in those days had greater financial and lawmaking powers within their states than did the members of Congress in the national government. Yet in forcing the Senate to be selected by the state legislature through the US Constitution inadvertently mandates the existence of a state legislature and thus forced the republic form of government upon each state. In the present age, most people rarely know anything about their state representatives and typically vote along straight party lines. I hope this discussion will shed some light on why the U.S.A. has no real name but is referenced as the United States because the nation itself was just considered a collection of individual states. Most nations are referenced by their cultural heritage identity, such as France, Spain, Russia, and so on, whereas in America, historically speaking, the only *true Americans* are those with a Native American heritage. Americans, by contrast, are referenced by their divided type of government, that is, the United *States*.

Nations of Laws, Not of Men[67]

The US Senate divides its responsibilities into various committees for managing the internal functionality of the federal government. Some of these committees include:

- Agriculture, Nutrition, and Forestry
- Banking, Housing and Urban Affairs
- Commerce, Science, and Transportation
- Health, Education, and Labor

Beyond that these departments are headed by advisors that report to the president who essentially functions as their CEO. Without a Senate how are the people to understand the fullness of the functionality of each department to put in place proposals to ensure their continual continuity? Our first solution is to divide these departments into individual realms each under the control of an elected shepherd. The shepherd by the nature of their position will see inefficiencies in the makeup and design of their realm. However, if a shepherd had the right to alter the laws governing their realm that may influence the shepherd's own authority and the checks and balances thereof, and once again I encounter the ancient threat of the shepherd, like Napoleon, crowning himself as Emperor. As a check on their authority, unlike a president, a shepherd only represents his realm and does not have authority over the

[67] Jeremiah 17:5–6; Isaiah 2:22.

jurisdiction of the other realms to allow competition between realms to keep proper jurisdictions intact. Whereas in a republic a president has authority over all jurisdictions under the authority of the federal government. Therefore, while it may seem that these same shepherds are the ones responsible for binding the Kingdom together; in reality, it is the people, through the use of national law, that binds the whole nation together. Beyond that a Senator only receives committee assignments after being elected, thus they may or may not have any related experience to the departmental committee of which they have been assigned. Furthermore, seeing the functionality from the top and the bottom are very different perspectives and in my experience the view from the bottom through how a person is treated that means nothing to management is more accurate than the view of a Senator which only sees people on their best behavior.

Beyond that, as a person in a republic is limited to voting for a governor from the state to which they reside, in the democracy each person is limited to electing a shepherd from the realm where the passion of their heart resides. The choice allows them to align their very being within their government. In the current republic the president is expected to be a jack of all trades, which means he is an expert of none and because the public is electing the one president, they too during the election season become a jack of all trades and an expert of none. Through the specialization of the realm, the shepherd, and the population, the people truly become the experts. During the election debates, the questions will get more granulated, and the answers thus more thought out as they will be contained within all things related to the jurisdiction of the realm to which the candidates are running. As it is said the squeaky wheel gets the grease as people will generally migrate to the realms that are the least functional. This gives the shepherd the incentive to govern beyond a political party base, giving ear to all concerns. Thus, society is not united through the power of the national government, but rather through the voice of the people, all the people. With that transition comes a transition from a powerless population of observers to a population of active participants. Powerless observers create gods out of men who are worshipped through the power they yield and thus the public are manipulated through the national propaganda used to put those leaders in power, but active participants are empowered through their own internal God given passions and to empower those passions and remove the obstacles is to unleash the limitless power of the Human Spirit.

Any one department or any position of authority in any government carries within itself the threat of taking away power and authority from the people, and therefore has the potential of undermining the direct-democracy itself. We must hold our leaders to a higher standard than we would the cast-aside person on the street. As the adage goes, "To whom much is given, much is required." Public officials are the servants of society. Servants always have fewer rights than their masters. The government is the servant of the people. Therefore, it stands to reason that those in authority have fewer rights than the people over whom they exert power and influence. For this reason, it is vital that whoever has strong authority over others—from district attorneys and judges to the police, military officers, and our elected officials—all must have a transparent existence, as much as possible, for in this way the people may have real trust that their decisions are being made on behalf of the public good.[68] For example, the average person in society has the right to have their financial transactions kept private. However, it may be vital to let the public know where a judge or an elected public servant is putting his or her finances or from whom they are borrowing or otherwise receiving substantial sums of money. By setting limitations on the rights of those in authority, society ensures justice for all, with a level playing field. On Election Day, people often vote on the outward appearance,[69] because people don't know the real heart of a person.[70] History has shown that those who wield authority have often been able to use the powers of their office corruptly, to augment themselves, acquiring more rights and powers than the cast-aside person, and doing so illegitimately. Of course, there must be limitations to transparency, but history has shown time and time again that the leaders of society have been themselves the most frequent sources of the evilest corruption, violence, and abuse of power.

Direct-democracy is made up of local governments (which consist of cities and shires), realms (e.g., Department of Transportation, Department of Agriculture, etc.), and a national government (military and foreign relations). Thus, following in the words of Thomas Jefferson, "My general plan would be, make the States one as to everything connected with foreign nations, and several as to everything purely domestic." To ensure leadership is subordinate to the people, lords are elected on the city and shepherds are elected on a realm level, but the law creation process takes place on the shire level, which encompasses all the lords in each shire and national level which encompasses all realms. The law enforcement process, on the other hand, remains on a city and state or realm level so that those in authority will remain always under or beneath the law rather than above the law. By creating laws on the shire level instead of the city level, the laws of the Shire may be used to unite the cities rather than uniting the people under their elected officials and politicians, which is the case in both the republics and the monarchic forms of government. This means that the lords of the individual cities in that shire remain under the shire law because the law itself—rather than a person, the lord—has the responsibility for uniting and ensuring teamwork and governmental cooperation within each shire. On the national level, we have expanded this concept to use the national laws to tie the states together and to ensure that the individual shepherds will remain always properly subordinate to the national laws.

The rights normally found within the states are now embodied in the shire (county) government. By removing the existence of the large state governments there is no more state law. By removing this large section of government from the equation a stronger bond between the shires and the realm/national government is created because there is no more middleman level of state government. As you will also see international law is now directly tied to the national government. Thus, you have two branches of government city/shire and national/international. Compare this with the Republic that requires a step up from person to city, from city to county, from county

---

[68] Political Corruption, Transparency International, <transparency.org/global_priorities/corruption_politics>.

[69] Samuel 10:23–24.

[70] Samuel 16:7.

to state, from state to federal, and then from federal to international. By the time leadership climbs the ladder to the top the people are so far removed from the equation that their relevance to it is lost.

According to the Republic there are three equal and separate parts of government: the courts, the legislature, and the president. However, this is not the case in a democracy because the people are always at the top of the chain and intersect on every level as the law creation body of the nation. Below the people exist the courts to ensure that the law enforce aka executive branch remains accountable to the people. The lowest level of government is therefore the executive branch because the executive branch is the greatest danger to usurping the rights of the people and thus undermining the democracy. To ensure that the courts have superior authority to the executive branches, but yet remains below the people, the court system, while it is established at city, realm, and national levels, the court system functions at a shire, national, constitutional, and foreign or international level. By having the city judges confirmed by the Shire Fellowship, which is made up of all the lords under the shire's jurisdiction, the city courts are rendering a shire level verdict are thus above the city lords to keep the lords accountable, always, to the shire laws, which are those passed by the people. This means that there are no shire courts, but only city courts that enforce shire laws. City courts are also made for criminal and civil cases in addition to cases levied against the lord or a member of a city's law enforcement agency, the local police. The city judges, while confirmed by the Shire Fellowship, are appointed by the lord's political opponents to not only keep the lord under the authority of the law but also to ensure the rights of the people living in the city who did not vote for a sitting lord.

To ensure the rights of the minority, the same path is followed on a national level. The National Court judges are not to be selected by the shepherd, but rather only by those who have the responsibility to investigate the shepherd, which is the Guardian, and then only the Roundtable approves the judge. In this way, these National Judges have authority derived from a national level, which places their authority on a higher-level than that of the shepherd.[71] This gives the National Court a national voice so that court also functions and acts as the federal court, as you know it in a republic. When there is a case between two realms, the prosecuting attorney will have to go to the National Court of the defending party. This achieves several objectives: first, the defending party, if it loses the case, will be losing to judges from its own realm. Second, by having the judge confirmed by the Roundtable, we ensure that the shepherds and the lords are kept accountable to the law, as individually they are lower in authority than the judges themselves are. As the adage goes, "No one is above the law," and remember, in this new form of government, the law is derived by, for and from the people. The court system also needs its own special checks and balances system, to ensure that it too remains accountable to the people.

---

[71] Hebrews 7:7-10.

Constitutions

Every machine is built upon various parts to fulfill different purposes that allow it to function successfully. In a car, for instance, is more than an engine, it functionality also needs a carburetor, radiator, and other gears essential to its operation. If any of these parts fail to perform the machine does not function. Not only for inorganic machinery, but also for all forms of life, from the small ameba to each of us as human-beings, should one vital organ cease to function life itself comes to a halt. The mechanics of government system is defined by its constitution. If the constitution is altered, perhaps with the best of intentions, if it does not fit properly within the anatomy of the system, the system itself risks upheaval and collapse. On the other side of the coin, there are equal risks in denying the natural evolution of government. The Ford corporation was the inventor of the Model-T, a revolution for its time, but by all accounts, today's Ford Mustang is technologically superior. As constitutions are considering foundational, unchanging cornerstone of any government, one must come to terms with a new reality that I am not proposing a new direct-democracy Constitution, but rather, the Jezreel, *Orb of Love,* is the architectural machine for government apparatus. The difference being that the Jezreel *Orb of Love,* is intended to be an evolving organic machine, a life, living and breathing through humanity, rather than the concrete system, cold and unchanging for all eternity as constitutions have become to be viewed. Beyond the normal laws passed by Congress there also exists constitutional amendments. Amendments can alter the general framework of the constitution and thus require larger majorities to pass. Amendments may also require ratification through the state legislatures. Thus, in a Republic the governed are divorced from the constitutional amendment process. To grant more power to the people, power must be correspondingly diminished from the federal and state governments. Because the federal government and state governments, who will never voluntarily relinquish their power, have the reigns over the constitutional amendment process, and the people have no say, the people have no hope of evolving into a democracy without revolutionary measures. Without an amendment process that allows the people to force change upon their government, to demand greater representation and liberty, the existing constitution is championed by the people because what little power they have is retained through their constitution. However, when the people become the Congress, it is right and proper for them to force change upon their leaders as they see fit to preserve the democracy and keep their leaders in check. It also remains hypocritical to have a government, of, by, and for the people, that denies the people the ultimate power to evolve the *Orb of Love* as they so desire.

On the other side of the equation, the greater the change to the system of government, the greater the risk that the system as designed may cease to function holistically with all its subcomponents. Therefore, our priority is to rate the amount of change in every national proposal put forward. During the Causa Enim Nova trial, each proposal will be given a rank by the jury as to the amount a change the proposal will introduce into the system. Starting with a rank of one, being a minor change, to a rank of ten being a full-blown revolution. As proposals go through the process, if two proposals merge the new proposal will take the higher of the two ranks, such that if a proposal with a change-rating of two merges with a proposal with a change-rating of five, the new proposals will have a score of five. Of course, proposals, as you have read, are also intended to evolve on their way to the ballot box so that during the Constitutional trial, a new score will be determined by the court. Like all proposals, the proposals with the greatest number of signatures from the public will make it to the ballot box, regardless of the change-rank, however, the greater the change, the greater the risk to the *Love Orb*, therefore the number of proposals on the ballot will be dictated by the proposal on the ballot with the highest change-rating. Fewer proposals mean that each proposal will receive the maximum amount of scrutiny by the public. So that, for instance, a proposal with a rank of ten, *Revolution Rank,* will be the only proposal on the ballot, so that the public can thoroughly discuss that proposal. We have restricted unconstitutional proposals from the local shire ballot so that when constitutional change takes place, all shires are affected equally, and no shire is adversely separated from the Jezreel, *Love Orb* system of government.

The law itself originated with the Torah of God as recorded by the hand of Moses. Every Sabbath the people were commanded to read the law of God, that is to say, the Word,[72] by the house of Aaron[73] so that the people may meditate on it.[74] Because the law was given by God, it was considered unchanging and therefore had a certain constitutional element and fundamental for societal structure and functionality. This leads us to the historical conflict between the Moralist who sees the law, the Word, and the constitution as concrete and unchanging, while the Humanist's direct aim and goal is the evolution of humanity through laws self-imposed that evolve through, by, and for humanity. However, our goal must be to meet both needs. On one end of the equation, we have laws written by humanity. Yet to be human is to be fallible. To have unintended consequences that the writers did not fathom. On the other end of the equation is love. It is the universal love through which in its pure form is always right and always just. As Paul stated love is the sum of all the law. Yet the determination of unfathomable love is through fallible human beings. Thus, I attempted to explain this COEXIST philosophical missing element in the moralist section of this work. Our greatest hope of evolution is when the two become one and indivisible. The enlightenment of humanity through the union of the moralist and the humanist. Therefore, while the Jezreel government exists under laws set up by and through humanity, the House of God courts remains the highest court of the land, whose underlying basis of legal interpretation is divine love and the foundational core of Jezreel, the constitution of Law of Love, as if it was, by which all laws are measured against. Consider, when the High Priest and the Levites with all their centuries of studying the law condemned Christ to the cross, Pontus Pilot could plainly see that he was innocent and washed his hands of the whole affair. His determination was not on the basis of written law, but the innate understanding of right and wrong within each of us. A reminder that the House of God of David in Jerusalem and the House of God of Jacob in Bethel, operate and function differently. The first through which Christ was convicted was based on the Tree of the Knowledge of Good and Evil, whose

---

[72] (The people) Deuteronomy 31:9–13; Josh 8:33–35; Nehemiah 8; Acts 15:21.(shepherds & leaders) Deuteronomy 17:18–19; 2 Kings 15:8–13.

[73] Psalms 119:89–91.

[74] Joshua 1:8; Psalms 1:2, 119:97.

fruit is judgment but the second coming temple of Bethel is based on the Tree of Life, of whose fruit is love, joy, peace, patience, kindness, goodness, faithfulness, gentleness, and self-control.[75] Therefore, there remains a Zadok Priestly set of courts in the temple[76] to see if any law directly violates the Divine love as a standard by which humanity's laws are measured against. It is important to recognize that not all court cases will be able to render a verdict based upon the existing law because the existing laws written by men does not have the divine ability to see the future yet love in its nature transcends time. In the existing court system, this turns judges into lawmakers, as they have no option, but to render a verdict based upon their own opinion in the absence of existing law. The priestly courts are to be used in domestic cases in the clear absence of pre-existing law as determined by the national court, as it is written:

> If cases come before your courts that are too difficult for you to judge —whether bloodshed, lawsuits or assaults —take them to the place Love your God will choose. Go to the Levitical priests and to the judge who is in office at that time. Inquire of them, and they will give you the verdict. You must act according to the decisions they give you at the place Love will choose. Be careful to do everything they instruct you to do. Act according to whatever they teach you and the decisions they give you. Do not turn aside from what they tell you, to the right, or to the left. Anyone who shows contempt for the judge or for the priest who stands ministering there to Love your God is to be put to death. You must purge the evil from Israel. All the people will hear and be afraid, and will not be contemptuous again.[77]

These cases, because existing law does not exist and the interim need is immediate, these foundational beginnings of Jezreel will set a precedent and from time to time incorporate the laws of love are introduced into the laws of men. If the public find fault with the decision the people through the vote may establish new laws as they themselves see prudent, thus unlike a theocracy, even the priestly courts are still accountable to the people.

I have not forgotten that the priestly line of Aaron once enslaved the people through the law,[78] but as there is a revival and resurrection of the house of Joseph, there is a death and rebirth of the house of Aaron and the covenant of grace.[79] I cannot ask anyone to believe in the testimony of Joseph and then cast-aside the testimony and responsibilities granted to Levi.[80] For as Man and Woman, Father and Son, Judah and Israel, the two were designed to function in union as one so that one is incomplete and outside of the harmony of Love without the other.

Other than laws set in stone, i.e., the Ten Commandments[81], there is still, in the foundations of law, another authority that has the potential to cause more bondage and more harm than all the other kinds of law combined, and that authority is the Jezreel *Love Orb* itself, if framed through the concept of a constitution. Constitutions, while created by humanity and not the divine, have a vital purpose—they serve as the last line of defense against tyranny and oppression. The longer a Constitution stays in place, the more it becomes an integral and fully accepted part of that society. On

[75] Galatians 5:22-23.
[76] Deuteronomy 17:8-13; Zechariah 3:7.
[77] Deuteronomy 17:8-13.
[78] Matthew 23:4; Luke 11:46.
[79] Luke 10:25–28.
[80] Zechariah 3:7.
[81] Exodus 20.

the other hand, we know that those who wield power continually seek with the greatest ingenuity and determination imaginable for any loophole, or any way to bypass or circumvent the just restraints placed upon their behavior to prevent them from pushing beyond the established limitations of their office. Patrick Henry said it this way, "The Constitution is not an instrument for the government to restrain the people; it is an instrument for the people to restrain the government—lest it comes to dominate our lives and interests." As we shall document further throughout this book, the Constitution that created America as a vibrant and strong political entity no longer contains the same vital restraints on power that the original designers so wisely intended. The national public degrees also contain powers of authority over public officials as a vital part of this new government plan to restrain abuses of power by those in office. Even so, these ideas are based only on the most realistic study of political history, and at that after the fact, where we can now see clearly the challenges and issues that the original designers could barely imagine. History is not just the past, but it is what is generally known about the past, and it is constantly being written, revised, and rewritten, right now, just as you read these pages. So then, while you are reading these thoughts, even greater concepts are being tossed about, considered, reconsidered, and finally in some sense created. It is all a part of the struggle of humankind to improve upon and upgrade its situation and its opportunities, its total environment, and room to live. Without the capability to modify the government model that I have laid out for you, even with all these efforts, this form of government could, in the end, become the greatest limitation upon our liberties, by not allowing liberty to evolve and advance. Much foresight and many wise provisions are needed. This threat has led us to develop several methods by which the foundational document, which is the Constitution itself, might be slightly altered or even more fundamentally transformed.

There is something else about Constitutions that I personally do not particularly like. The first Constitution maybe was accepted by votes, but each generation that followed thereafter merely inherits the Constitution without ever actually having a voice in the foundation of its government. A government's Constitution is, in this case, something into which we are all born, and we have few means to alter. For this reason, on the bicentennial of the original ratification of this Constitution, once every fifty years, society will have a vote as to whether the Constitution as is should be accepted or rejected. With this one provision, at least once in most people's lifetimes, they could choose with their own vote either to accept or to reject the Constitution. This, too is in line with Jeffersonian philosophy who believed one generation did not have the authority to force a government on the next or succeeding generations. In the words of Jefferson: *We may consider each generation as a distinct nation, with a right, by the will of its majority, to bind themselves, but none to bind the succeeding generation, more than the inhabitants of another country.*[82]

Prophetically the day that Israel and Judah become one is the year of Jubilee, celebrated every forty-nine years. Therefore, it also represents the birth of the

---

[82] In Defense of Democracy, <etext.virginia.edu/jefferson/quotations/>; Letter to William Stevens Smith (November 13, 1787), quoted in Padover's *Jefferson on Democracy*, <en.wikiquote.org/wiki/Thomas_Jefferson>.

nation. For any nation, the Day of Independence or Birth is a day of great national pride. In the United States, every July 4, people are accustomed to celebrating their independence as a nation with fireworks, parades, music, and celebrations. It is also a time of reflection, evaluation, and reassessment, to look at where society has been and where it now seems to be headed. This gives each generation a chance to accept this government model as it is, and if they do not like it to ask for something else. How do we know for sure that something else might not be even better? The designers of the US Constitution were intelligent people, but the heart can create an aura around ideas that only time can reveal the reality of how those ideas play out. Each generation has superior eyes, to see the implementation of another's imagination in concrete terms. This book is in effect a proposal for Revolution with guidelines laid out of how a proposed revolution may be effectively created. Does such a vote for or against this Constitution mean anything if the people are not granted other constitutions to weigh this Constitution against? Ergo, if the Constitution is not accepted, the people have the right to vote on several Revolution proposals (The proposal with a change-rank of ten with the most signatures). Like Amendment proposals, people may also sponsor Revolution proposals and get cosponsors and signatures as they do for any other proposal or law. Therefore, during the year of Jubilee, the people can take a sabbatical to debate evolve Jezreel perpetually if they choose to do so and a large part of me hopes that they will.

Then again, if the people choose to retain their form of government (this one), then they will also have a second question to indicate whether they believe that the existing Constitution is being enforced as was originally intended. This vote is designed in such a way as to grant a voice and an open-door to see where corruption through the ways of tyrants may have diminished or damaged the voice of the people. It is yet another of those necessary checks on the powers that be.

If the existing Constitution for the Jezreel is approved, all proposed amendments to the democracy older than the day of the last 20-year election will be dissolved, and the fireworks may begin.

Finally, as the Architect of Jezreel, most of the ideas presented to humanity are built upon a working theory and hypothesis regarding how things work. My knowledge of the system in many ways is unique from that of the reader, as the originator of the ideas. In the past, I worked in product management, quality assurance, and technical support and the one important lesson that I learned was that a person and a company could test and re-test and believe they have everything perfect, but when you send the product out to the real-world, only at that point does reality meet theory and only then can a true evaluation be determined. Having said that there are lessons that I can only learn through seeing this new system in action. Yet I am only given so many days in this life. Shall we ask the founding fathers their opinion of the Constitution they ratified, what changes they would make today? If only we could, but they are dead and gone. Considering that after the passage of the Love Orb, I will be making notes, seeing its successes and failures of that initial era. One year after my passing my final version will be offered to the public through the course of a normal initiative on the ballot. This is my final sunset.

A Final Defense

Sadly the application of even the most essential rights can be misused to allow the worst of atrocities. Under the guise of freedom of the press and freedom of speech, people will plant hidden cameras in toilets to take lewd pictures and post them on the internet. Women will put trust in the wrong man, allowing him to take photos of herself in the context of a relationship and later when the relationship is over the photos are used for extortion or published online for the sole purpose of degrading causing her shame. Famous actors have paparazzi looking for explicit moments in their private life for profit and gain. I must believe that James Madison designed the bill of rights to support freedom of speech and the press he had greater things in mind than this. Each person has a right to their sexual privacy, and the rights between two people in a relationship with each other are changed should the relationship end. Outside of the context of love there becomes endless exceptions to every rule thus laws are written on top of laws endlessly until the law becomes so convoluted that it is impossible for even the best minds to see it in its fullness. We must allow the public to enforce the law of love when the law is construed to allow evil for which its authors did not contemplate. To accomplish this, I am thus allowing the jury to make a *Declaration of Common Sense.* If the jury believes that the law or its application is unjustifiable or wrong, the jury retains the right to acquit the defendant if they believe that the defendant was acting in a justifiable manner through rational common sense. The law must never deny the people the morality to behave in a manner that they believe to be morally right and justified. After all, a Democracy has been created for rational humanity, not obedient lemmings. Often circumstances justify the breaking of a just law, where the law writers are unable to see the specific circumstances of every application. A friend of mine was in the World Trade Center in New York on Sept 11, 2001. The police would not let anyone leave through the front doors for fear that a jumper from above would land on them. He hit the police officer and, taking his niece by the hand, forced his way out the front door. The building collapsed behind him. He and his niece were the last ones to make it out of the building alive. Those who were obedient to the law died through their obedience. Would it be right to prosecute him for his defiance or for assaulting a police officer? The government is often looking for blind obedience, and often prosecutors do not consider the circumstances behind the act, but rather only the act itself. Each time the jury issues a verdict of Declaration of Common Sense, it will be noted and tabled for future law-creation as well as grading system of sorts to keep our law creators in check.

The three greatest vices in humanity are wealth, fame, and power. It is this eternal craving which is never satisfied that transforms leaders into despots. In a republic, Congress was partially developed to keep the president in check, the state legislature to keep the governor in check, and all the way down to the city council, to keep the mayor in check. In this new government, there is no Congress in the conventional sense. Still, we must have strict methods of enforcement that maintain controls over our leaders, thus preventing them from crowning themselves as kings or absolute monarchs while also allowing them to exercise their legitimate powers of direction and control. Also, without effective enforcement, laws become meaningless. Thus, I am tasked with creating and molding the right kind of leadership to unleash the human spirit and take humanity to the next level.

The leaders we follow say a lot about us. I went to my pastor and told him one can interpret the Bible in a fundamentalist way to show that God has a Divine purpose behind all faiths and intends to use our religious diversity to make humanity one. He laughed and told me I was dreaming. I went to my college political science professor and told him that Direct Democracy is not only practical, but the only realistic solution to bring a voice to the billions left unheard. He too laughed and told me I had read too many fairytales. Both lacked the time and patience to hear my solution because they were already convinced it was not possible and yet hear you see I have laid out both solutions in practical and realistic ways. In the next section dedicated to the capitalist I am going to privatize the government. I will let you guess what the response was from my economics professor. Despite all the beauty of our dreams their remains safety in the things we know. This is why the prophets were always persecuted because change is an unknown world. Israel was enslaved in Egypt for four hundred years always knowing the promised land was their destiny, yet when God commanded them to enter the Land through Joshua and Caleb the leaders of the ten other tribes told the people we are better off as slaves and the people believed them to such a degree that they tried to murder God's two witnesses. Two vails have now been removed. You, the reader, have had the courage to make it this far. Is your heart prepared to turn the page? Can you see the Promised Land beginning to form? Do you hear the call of the Piper's flute? This is the world of the Capitalist, the roar of the warrior against all odds standing with the two in opposition to the ten. Destiny is calling!

www.ingramcontent.com/pod-product-compliance
Lightning Source LLC
Chambersburg PA
CBHW080427290526
45791CB00008BA/2419

* 9 7 8 1 3 0 0 8 7 7 8 2 0 *